MONEYBALL FOR GOVERNMENT

SECOND EDITION

MONEYBALL FOR GOVERNMENT

SECOND EDITION

Edited by Former Congressman Jim Nussle and Peter Orszag

with U.S. Senator Kelly Ayotte and U.S. Senator Mark Warner

and Glenn Hubbard
Gene Sperling
Melody Barnes
John Bridgeland
Kevin Madden
Howard Wolfson
Michael Gerson
Raj Shah
Robert Gordon
Ron Haskins

**DISRUPTION
BOOKS**

Published in the United States of America by Disruption Books.

ISBN 978-1-63331-003-2

Printed in the United States of America

Design by Studio Kudos

Second Edition

Because of the extraordinary work of so many nonprofits and researchers, we now know more than ever before about what works to help young people, their families, and communities succeed and flourish in America today. Social entrepreneurs, academics, governments at all levels—and even entire communities—have figured out ways to increase opportunity, foster social mobility, and lift the lives of Americans most in need.

If a child is born into a family whose income is in the bottom 25 percent of U.S. earners, she is going to experience distressingly little social mobility without the right kind of supports and networks we all have needed to succeed in life. This includes getting a quality early education; attending a strong elementary school that ensures she is reading at grade level by the third grade and has strong math skills by eighth grade; staying on track to graduate from high school, with the right mentors and guidance to overcome challenges; attending either college or work training; and getting a second chance if she does get off track.[1]

But too often, having a better sense of what works has not necessarily translated into policy makers and elected officials using this information to inform policy and funding choices. And, in many cases, there is an enormous disconnect between knowing what we need to do and knowing whether we've done it right. It's one thing to know that early education should be an investment priority; it's another to know whether the preschool program we fund is effective. There also is significantly more that can—and must—be learned, especially with the rapid changes in our economy and society. It is a continuous process of figuring out what works for whom and in what circumstances.

Without building more knowledge about what works and changing the way that government allocates resources, it will be impossible to make large-scale progress on the most significant challenges facing kids and their families. And that's what this book is all about: dramatically expanding opportunity by making sure that policy and funding decisions by governments at all levels are informed by the best possible data and evidence about impact.

If we can bridge that gap between knowing what needs to be done and elected officials and policy makers using that information to make better choices, then we can make great leaps in the results government gets from its investments. And it will create new incentives for nonprofits and providers to build and use evidence to improve impact, creating a pipeline of new, evidence-based approaches.

We believe this can be achieved in a bipartisan way. For proof, look no further than the great leaders and thinkers—from both sides of the aisle—who have joined together for this project. They are truly a Who's Who from across the political spectrum.

You'll hear from Senator Kelly Ayotte, a Republican from New Hampshire, and Senator Mark Warner, a Democrat from Virginia.

You'll hear from some of the most senior leaders from the Obama and Bush White Houses: Peter Orszag and Jim Nussle, who led President Obama's and President Bush's Office of Management and Budget, respectively; Melody Barnes and John Bridgeland, directors of the White House Domestic Policy Council under Presidents Obama and Bush, respectively; Gene Sperling, who served as chief economic adviser to both Presidents Clinton and Obama; and

Glenn Hubbard, who was President Bush's chief economist at the White House Council of Economic Advisers.

You'll hear from political strategists: Howard Wolfson, who advised Hillary Clinton's 2008 presidential campaign and served as deputy mayor of New York under Mayor Michael Bloomberg; and Kevin Madden, who advised Mitt Romney's presidential campaigns in 2008 and 2012. And at the end of the book, you can read about a bipartisan Moneyball agenda, which was crafted by Robert Gordon, a former Obama policy adviser, and Ron Haskins, a former Bush policy adviser.

The path laid out in the following pages offers a way to make a tremendous impact on social outcomes in America. And that truly matters. Because while this book might concern itself largely with budgets and data, our real subject—our true purpose—is how we can create opportunities for all Americans.

This effort will not be easy. The challenges facing our communities are complex. And there will always be judgment calls about how to interpret and use data and evidence. But the authors of this book believe, rightfully, that we can achieve something substantial for the American people if more and better information is used to guide the vital investments our nation makes in young people, their families, and communities. We hope you agree. And if you do, we hope you'll join us in the quest to make this a reality.

Michele Jolin
Founder and Managing Partner of Results for America

MONEYBALL
FOR GOVERNMENT

Chapter I.

LET'S PLAY MONEYBALL

By **Former Congressman Jim Nussle (R-IA)**
OMB director under President George W. Bush and former
U.S. House Budget Committee chair

Peter Orszag
OMB director under President Barack Obama

Between August 13 and September 4, 2002, the Oakland Athletics baseball team didn't lose a single time. For twenty consecutive games—an American League record—a team of misfits and overlooked talent dominated Major League Baseball like never before. And they did so, incredibly, on a budget of just $40 million—less than a third that of the league's richest teams.

Oakland's success came about not in spite of their measly resources but because of them. Recognizing that his team could never compete in a system where only the wealthiest could be winners, Billy Beane, the team's general manager, began identifying and exploiting inefficiencies in the game that other teams had missed. He embraced his team's scarce resources and let statistics, not unscientific scouting reports, drive his draft picks. The rest of the league could play baseball; Billy Beane and the Oakland A's were playing "Moneyball."

It's a compelling story, especially in the hands of a writer like Michael Lewis, who coined the term and penned the 2003 bestselling book of that name.' At its heart, Moneyball is about crunching numbers and relying on hard evidence—not emotion or tradition—to drive decisions about how to allocate scarce resources. It's also about determining what data matter and what don't (in the case of baseball, concluding that on-base percentage matters a lot more than total home runs). When it comes down to it, it's a way to get more with less.

Which raises important questions: Can data, evidence, and evaluation similarly revolutionize America's government? Can we provide better services to millions more Americans while actually saving billions of dollars? Can we make this country a better place for children and families by investing in what works, by testing it and retesting it, and by holding ourselves to a higher standard? In short, can government play Moneyball?

The answer, we believe, is a resounding yes.[3]

It might seem obvious that the government, which collects more than $2.4 trillion in taxes each year (and spends more than $3 trillion), would want to know whether it is spending that money effectively.[4] But too often we lack the answer to that very important question. In fact, astonishingly, based on our estimate, less than one dollar out of every hundred dollars the federal government spends is backed by even the most basic evidence. We might know a program is popular. We might even see data that suggest the program is performing efficiently. But it is the relatively rare case when we actually have the evidence to tell us a program is working as intended and it's the most effective way to achieve the outcome we desire.

Federal programs might be working; but in too many cases, we just don't know. With the mounting challenges our nation is facing, it is not enough to base government spending on intuition, instinct, or—the overwhelming rationale for most programs— what has been funded in the past. That is especially important given that, very often, when we do investigate the efficacy of federal programs, the results are not encouraging. Since 1990, the federal government has rigorously tested ten large social programs through randomized controlled trials (RCTs), the gold standard of evaluation. Of the ten programs—which collectively cost taxpayers over $10 billion annually—nine showed "weak or no positive effects" on their participants.

This would be a problem under any circumstance—after all, as former Senate minority leader Everett Dirksen is famously said to have remarked, "A billion here, a billion there, and pretty soon you're talking real money." But in the wake of the 2008 recession and recent budget agreements—with jobs and GDP growing modestly, discretionary spending under tight caps, and cash-strapped governments struggling to do more with less—it's even more critical that we maximize the impact of every taxpayer dollar we invest.

Ultimately, this is a debate about genuinely improving the lives of children and their parents by making sure we are spending our resources in the right way. And while these debates tend to play out in the abstract language of dollars and cents, the impact is not merely seen in columns in an Excel spreadsheet or line items in an omnibus budget bill. Our failure to assess the effectiveness of government spending carries more than a financial cost—it has a massive human cost as well. When a program designed to boost employment fails to perform, parents are unable to put food on their families' tables. When an education initiative doesn't live up to its promise, neither can the young children enrolled in it.

Fortunately, it doesn't have to be this way. Thanks to decades of social-science research, we know more about how to help struggling Americans than ever before. And in this era of impact-blind, across-the-board budget cuts, we see an opportunity. Like Billy Beane and the A's, these lean times offer us a chance to reevaluate how we measure success and to shift our focus to what works.

First, we need to change the debate—to focus at least as much on the quality of resources as the quantity. Our goal is to get policy makers to adopt three principles that we believe can improve outcomes for young people, their families, and their communities:

1. Build evidence about the practices, policies, and programs that will achieve the most effective and efficient results.

2. Invest limited taxpayer dollars in practices, policies, and programs that use evidence and evaluation to demonstrate that they work.

3. Direct funds away from practices, policies, and programs that consistently fail to achieve measurable outcomes.

The good news is, the government has already begun to play Moneyball in some areas. During the administration of President George W. Bush—America's first MBA president as well as a former Major League Baseball–team owner—the Office of Management and Budget (OMB) developed a Program Assessment Rating Tool (PART) to evaluate social programs and adjust funding according to their success. The Obama administration took up the baton in 2009 and has since become the most evidence-based administration in history.[5]

Take, for example, the popular Head Start program, which spends $8 billion annually providing early-childhood education, health, and nutrition assistance to nearly a million disadvantaged children. Ever since it was created in 1965, politicians and researchers have studied and debated its effectiveness. Supporters pointed to math and literacy gains, while critics noted that those improvements disappeared in elementary school.

In 2007, President Bush signed a law that required all Head Start grantees to be evaluated using an evidence-based system. President Obama has since initiated a series of targeted reforms to weed out underperforming providers and has refused to automatically fund about one-third of programs. In order to re-qualify, they would have to improve.

To be sure, the evidence-based agenda we are proposing isn't just about identifying programs that aren't working; it's about scaling up those that are, and improving those that show promise. Consider Nurse-Family Partnership, one of the best examples of evidence in action.[6] Early in his career, David Olds worked at a day-care center in inner-city Baltimore, where he hoped to change the lives of low-income children. But to his frustration, he found that, even by preschool age, many of the children he worked with were already at an enormous developmental and educational disadvantage. Rather than give up, David changed his approach, deciding to focus his efforts even earlier—in some cases, before the child is even born.

He created an organization called Nurse-Family Partnership, which sends nurses to the homes of first-time, low-income mothers and their children. There they would help women prepare for everything from the birth itself to raising a baby, planning future pregnancies, staying in school, and preparing for the workforce.

"When a woman becomes pregnant, whether she's fourteen or forty, there's a window of opportunity," explained Valerie Carberry, a nurse for the program. "They want to do what's right. They want to change bad behaviors—tobacco, alcohol, using a seat belt, anything. As nurses, we're able to come in and become part of their lives; it's a golden moment."

But Olds did more than build Nurse-Family Partnership; he did the rigorous evaluation to prove it would work. Over the next thirty years, he tested the program in randomized trials in three different communities. His results showed that the program was a remarkable success—improving pregnancy outcomes, bolstering the health and development of children, and helping parents create a positive life course for themselves. He took that evidence and the support of modest private funding to scale his program, from just a few locations to more than forty states by 2013. And in proving the effectiveness of the program, the organization was able to help secure a $1.5 billion federal investment in similar programs around the country. That funding was set to expire in 2014, but Congress has extended the program once already on a bipartisan basis and is likely to do so again in the future. Home visitation is a great example of building political support the right way—by doing what works.

The move toward more analytical policy making is encouraging. From the Obama administration's Social Innovation Fund to New York City's Center for Economic Opportunity, we are seeing more and more examples of policy making based on data and evidence that makes a meaningful impact.

We're not naïve: we know from personal experience that overhauling how the federal government does business isn't easy. While local, state, and federal governments have made positive strides, scaling up a handful of promising pilot programs into a completely reimagined framework for governance presents some real challenges.

For one thing, policy makers' incentives aren't always aligned with the imperative to squeeze the most impact out of every dollar. Sometimes politicians oppose reform for nefarious reasons—to protect a special interest or a major donor, for example. Sometimes they protect a program because of who started it, whose pet project it was, rather than whether it's working. For too many members of Congress, when it comes to evidence, it's just easier not to know.

All of that is before you consider our current political environment, which is, to put it charitably, not particularly conducive to making major changes. In truth, it's downright dysfunctional— so polarized and toxic that Democrats and Republicans can hardly stand to be in the same room together, let alone overhaul our approach to governance. And in the rare instances when our elected officials manage to forge bipartisan consensus, legislation is still often blocked for petty political reasons. To anyone watching the current mess in Washington, it's not surprising that from 2011 to 2013, Congress passed fewer bills than any Congress in more than half a century.[7]

But while the obstacles to evidence-based governance are formidable, they are not insurmountable. In fact, there are a number of good reasons to be optimistic.

First, there is a political opportunity for both parties. Republicans will have the chance not only to identify and eliminate real waste in the system but also to prove that a smaller government can be a more effective government. Democrats, on the other hand, will be able to fine-tune government until it is smarter and works better, and leverage it to better deliver services to vulnerable populations. There is nothing ideological about this approach, which is why we've already seen broad bipartisan support for these ideas.

Second, there is an economic opportunity. Researchers have projected, for example, that closing the achievement gap would boost GDP by 3 to 5 percent.[8] By collecting—and then leveraging—evidence to improve the way we approach this challenging problem, we can dramatically improve our economic footing.

Already, we've witnessed policy makers seizing these opportunities. In Texas and many other states, where the prison systems are straining budgets, die-hard conservative Republicans have joined with Democrats to reform the state's criminal-justice system.[9] This has saved money (a Republican priority) while simultaneously creating humane alternatives to incarceration (a longtime goal for Democrats).

Finally, there is a moral opportunity. Regardless of party, those who work in government do so because they care about helping their fellow citizens. And right now, we're not doing all that we could be. Half of low-income fourth graders aren't even reading at a basic level—yet we know there are proven ways to change that.[10] One out of every fifteen African American men is in jail—yet we know that good evidence can change that, too.[11] So let's build that evidence, analyze it, and use it as a tool to do a better job of running this country.

That, in a nutshell, is the case for Moneyball. It might sound like a basic idea, but it's also a big idea. As Billy Beane explained to Peter Brand, his prized statistician, "If we win, on our budget, with this team . . . we'll have changed the game. And that's what I want." That's what we want as well: to change the game, to get government working better, and to brighten the opportunity of and possibilities for everyone who calls America home.

So, ladies and gentlemen, let's play Moneyball.

Chapter II.

THE PURSUIT OF EVIDENCE

By   **Glenn Hubbard**
Chairman of the Council of Economic Advisers under
President George W. Bush

Economists disagree about many things, but one thing we know is that economic growth depends on much more than saving and investment, though these factors are important. If people are better educated and healthier, they are going to be more productive and earn more, too. Economists may not spend a lot of time designing school systems or public-health campaigns, but we know that their success is critical to a nation's wealth and well-being.

But believing that social interventions matter and knowing how to improve them are fundamentally different things. Unfortunately, policy makers often identify important points of intervention but fail to rigorously determine the most efficient and effective way to make them. In some cases, we have spent decades funding programs without ever evaluating whether they are working as intended. Sometimes that means we are funding programs that don't work, creating an opportunity cost for the populations enrolled in it and generating a net-negative impact on the economy.

The key to improving the performance of social programs is to better understand what works and what doesn't. In other fields of endeavor, from medicine to economics, we've improved our understanding by applying scientific methods. Thankfully, we are increasingly doing the same when it comes to social programs.

But even if we find broad consensus around the necessity to play Moneyball, there are still challenges to how we collect data and how we analyze data as evidence. In this chapter, I will describe what those challenges are and outline some of the ways that policy makers have already begun implementing processes that allow for rigorous, scalable evaluation.

DATA AND EVIDENCE

Before we go further, we should define two key terms that are often used interchangeably but mean different things: *data* and *evidence*.

When we say that the government lacks evidence that many of its programs work, we don't mean that it lacks data on those programs. We collect a lot of data. We live in a world with so much data that it now comes in categories: big data, open data, metadata, and so on. When it comes to government programs, we often have a lot of data about what they cost or how many people they employ— what are often called *inputs*. We may also know how many people they serve and in what ways—often named *outputs*. The trouble is that these data don't tell us much about how the program is (or isn't) changing people's lives.

In recent years we've gotten better about tracking *outcomes*— that is, not how many kids are served by a tutoring program but how those kids are performing in school as a result of that program. This step toward usable evidence is a big one—that is, data that actually support (or reject) a given argument or hypothesis. In the context of government programs, it is the information that helps us assess whether a program is working.

But finding evidence is not as simple as sifting through existing data (though, in certain cases, this may prove fruitful).

Evidence that a program works, ultimately, requires an understanding of what outcomes would have occurred in the program's absence. It's the only way to know whether a student's improvement is because of the tutoring program or because of other factors.

Consider a program like class-size reduction, an initiative that has been tried in multiple states in an effort to improve education outcomes. The states collect a lot of data on the program. We might know, for example, that there are ten third-grade classrooms in a given school district that have a maximum of twenty kids in them; that 95 percent of the students in those classes are reading at grade level; that 75 percent of students who had a reduced class size in third grade went on to graduate from high school; and so on.

Those data appear to be clear evidence that the program is working. But our perception of what these data confirm, and what they actually confirm, might be different.

It could be the case, for example, that the students are meeting reading levels not because of smaller class sizes but because of an enrichment-reading program that local parents run after school. It could be that the district is located in an affluent suburb where high salaries and low housing costs attract some of the highest-performing teachers to the state—teachers who are able to achieve the same outcome whether they have classes of twenty or thirty. In short, it is very possible that class-size reduction actually had no impact on the data that were collected on behalf of the program and that will surely be used to promote it.

The only certain way to know if a given program (in this case class-size reduction) had its intended impact is to know how a program participant would have fared in the absence of the program. That is, we need to know what would have happened to that very same third grader had she ended up in a larger class.

Strictly speaking, it is not possible to answer that question. Everything in the world happens the way it happens, not some other way. A struggling entrepreneur either receives a government loan or she doesn't. A worker goes through a job-training program or he doesn't. A student enrolls in a small class or she doesn't.

This represents the core challenge of evaluating the impact of a given government program. Proving the *causal* effects of a program seems to require something more.

So how do we resolve this challenge? How do we develop impact evaluations that can successfully establish whether a program is causing an impact?

IMPACT EVALUATIONS

When there's the opportunity, we approach our analysis the way a scientist would analyze data against her hypothesis: we conduct a randomized controlled trial.

Consider a medical researcher testing a new weight-loss pill. The researcher faces the same causal challenge we do: If you can't assess the same individual operating in two different realities (one in which he takes the pill and one in which he doesn't), how do you know whether the pill works? The answer is to randomly assign participants to two separate groups: a control group, which will not take the pill, and a treatment group, which will. By assigning people randomly to each group, differences among the patients (for example, education levels, weight, exercise habits, or medical history) should exist in roughly equal measure in each group. The only variable that changes between each group, then, is the new medication. The researcher can now measure the outcomes between the two groups and reasonably conclude that any difference was attributable to the pill.

Thirty years ago, Tennessee took exactly this approach to class-size reduction.[12] Starting in 1985, under Governor Lamar Alexander, students and teachers were randomly assigned to one of two types of classes: a regular class, with an average of twenty-three students, or a small class, with an average of fifteen students. The experiment lasted four years, so students were either in small or regular classes through third grade.

The study had a striking result: students in the smaller classes outperformed students in the regular classes by a significant amount, from the perspective of both statisticians and educators.[13] And as researchers have followed these students into adulthood, they've found that the students in small classes were likelier to go to college than students in the regular-sized classes.[14]

The randomized design in Tennessee rules out the possibility that the kids in smaller classes came from wealthier homes or had better teachers. That doesn't make it foolproof. For example, because the study wasn't double-blind like a medical research study, the teachers knew they were being studied. Some have speculated that this focus motivated the teachers in small classes to perform better, and point to studies, using other methods, that have found that class-size reduction doesn't have much of an impact.[15]

There's also a vigorous debate about whether class-size reduction is the right policy approach for kids. After all, Tennessee's class-size reduction cost thousands of dollars per child. Most school districts don't have that kind of money, and other investments may well have bigger bang for the buck.

Even so, these caveats shouldn't obscure the basic truth: because Tennessee went to the trouble of setting up a class-size experiment, we know this approach to improving schools can make a difference for young children. It's left to debate whether it will work in a particular case and whether it's worth the cost. But whatever choice we make will be informed by rigorous evidence. If we did comparable research on other key interventions, we'd be in a much better position to help kids learn.

Resources are limited, though, and we can't afford to give the most promising interventions to everyone who wants them. This is unfortunate, but it regularly creates a perfect research opportunity. If there are five hundred slots available in a new program, then instead of enrolling the first five hundred eligible people to sign up, we can let a thousand eligible people sign up, and hold a lottery to determine who among them participates. Just like that, we've created a randomized controlled trial. The people who got into the program will be no different, as a group, from the people who didn't, so we can zero in on the program's effects. Thanks to these kinds of lotteries, we're learning a lot about things like oversubscribed charter schools, for example.

Another frequently noted problem for the most rigorous kinds of research is cost. If you want to look at whether an intervention with troubled teenagers works, it used to be that you would need to interview teachers, school administrators, police officers, and community members, which was incredibly, often prohibitively expensive. Today researchers can use data that schools, health centers, and police officers already collect. A study that used to cost $1 million might now be pulled off for 20 percent less.

Still, the truth is that randomized trials aren't always feasible. If we aren't already collecting the data—as is usually the case with young children—those trials cost a lot. It rarely makes sense to run an expensive evaluation on a program that is just starting up. And even when we do have data, we can't always randomize, for either practical or ethical reasons. If you're trying to look at whether changing the rules for teacher tenure improves student outcomes, it's pretty hard to randomize which teachers get tenure under which rules. If you're interested in seeing whether individuals with lower unemployment benefits will find work faster, you can't set benefits at random.

For cases like these, social scientists have developed a number of alternative—and ingenious—ways to gather causal evidence on the impact of programs. One such approach is to simulate a genuine random experiment using the natural dividing lines between those who are eligible for a program and those who are not. Consider, for example, an attempt to determine whether Medicaid has effectively improved the health of the low-income individuals who are eligible for it. Rather than randomly dividing a group of Medicaid recipients into a treatment group and control group, researchers could evaluate the health outcomes of people who just barely meet the eligibility requirements of Medicaid and those who just barely miss the cutoff. If, for example, the Medicaid income-eligibility cutoff is 185 percent of the poverty line, we can be reasonably confident that people who earn 184 percent of the poverty line and those who earn 186 percent are the same in every way except one: access to Medicaid. Researchers could therefore gather data on the health outcomes of a random sampling from each group and use it to measure whether Medicaid really works.

There are some great recent examples of research that have used low-cost methods to study low-cost interventions that have turned out to make a real difference in people's lives. For example, if you put fresh fruit in a colorful bowl at the front of the cafeteria line, kids will eat more of it.[16] If you give college freshmen facing academic challenges a twenty-minute talk that reinforces the value of hard work and the possibility of success, they'll do better in classes. If you tell people who failed to pay their taxes that most other people *do* pay, they're likelier to pay up themselves. These are simple findings that social programs and government agencies can now act on.[17]

As in so many things, when it comes to evaluation, government has a lot to learn from the private sector. One way that businesses continually improve is by testing different approaches to their work, constantly, in real time, without much fuss. Leading banks and retailers are constantly testing different approaches to their work. An e-commerce site, for example, might "A/B test" different messages—"Offer ends soon!" versus "Offer ends Saturday!"—to randomly selected sample populations and see which performs better. Grocery stores experiment with putting different products in different places. Search engines test different colors. In fact, companies from eBay to Netflix—not to mention presidential campaigns with their endless (and endlessly tested) fund-raising e-mails—routinely run thousands of such randomized experiments.[18]

The same real-time testing that has revolutionized business could similarly transform the federal government. For example, a program to offer post-traumatic-stress-disorder therapy to veterans might be described in different ways at different Veterans Affairs hospitals, to measure which is most effective at producing sign-ups. An antismoking campaign could test its message to make sure it's most likely to reach at-risk young people. The Internal Revenue Service could continually test the best messages to ensure people file their taxes.

There is no doubt that gathering and evaluating evidence of impact in a complex world is challenging. At the same time, researchers and policy makers across government are already hard at work applying these approaches to build evidence for what works and what doesn't. They're coming to conclusions that are reducing homelessness and improving hospice care. They're simplifying financial-aid forms and boosting college enrollment for disadvantaged students. And they're showing that—with the right resources and a changing landscape that puts evidence-based policy front and center—it's possible to do more than *talk* about making government work better; we can evaluate the data and marshal the evidence to make it happen.

Chapter III.

A CONTINUUM APPROACH

By **Gene Sperling**
Director of the National Economic Council under
President Bill Clinton and President Barack Obama

Fixing a problem requires knowing what works. That makes the need for evidence-based policy making ever present, not just in fiscally constrained times but at all times. After all, if the goal of public policy is to *improve* lives and not just *appear* to be doing so, evidence is always helpful for knowing whether we are delivering on our good intentions.

Evidence also helps move people to action. Too often, advocates for a worthy cause rely on a two-step appeal: a powerful presentation of the problem followed by a vigorous call for action. Yet simply showing the vastness and severity of a problem does not, in and of itself, motivate effort and investment. At times, a passionate presentation that only demonstrates how terrible a problem is can leave policy makers—and the public as a whole—feeling as though the challenge is intractable, depressing, and hopeless.

In my experience, what motivates people to expend precious resources is a three-part appeal. It begins with the presentation of the problem and ends with the call to action, but the critical step is the middle one: clear proof that there are interventions that work but aren't in place on a sufficiently large scale. Such a clear demonstration of the potential for success is what creates the tension that leads citizens and policy makers to say, "If we know there are solutions that are working and could dramatically change more lives for the better, how can we fail to act?"

Nonetheless, even if we embrace rigorous evidence-based policy making, we will still at times—particularly in the short run—face a difficult challenge: How do we make decisions on pressing and even urgent policy issues impacting millions of people's lives when our information is imperfect and not based on the rigorous evidence we prefer?

A CONTINUUM VS. AN ON-OFF-SWITCH APPROACH

As Glenn described in the preceding chapter, there is no better form of evidence than the results of randomized controlled trials (RCTs). But often, policy makers have to make urgent decisions in the absence of such high-caliber evidence, which usually takes many years to gather.

In such circumstances, the key is to consider the kind of evidence that can inform policy decisions along a continuum. We must push fellow policy makers, nonprofits, and foundations to develop better evidence, including more RCTs, while at the same time relying on the best available evidence we currently have. As Glenn explained, there are often very rigorous research methods short of RCTs.

At the same time, we cannot afford to view an evidence-based approach as an on-off switch—where lack of evidence is used as a justification for shutting off all critical policy interventions to address pressing social and economic challenges. An evidence-based approach should never become a pretext to argue that if RCTs do not exist right now, we must turn our back and do nothing to address major economic and social injustices. A failure to use the best evidence available—to engage in what FDR called "bold experimentation"—would be tantamount to preserving an untenable status quo.

The better approach is to rely carefully on the best evidence available in the short run while simultaneously pushing for the development of more rigorous analysis. Major funding increases for programs that look promising but lack rigorous supporting research should be implemented in stages, under careful study, with requirements for high-quality evaluation, and with the capacity to course-correct along the way.

Throughout this process, it's also important to remember that while RCTs may be the gold standard of evidence, they are not infallible. Evaluations can be poorly designed, focusing on what is easy or quick to measure instead of what might be most important over time. It's like the old joke about looking for your lost keys under the lamppost because that's where the light is. An education intervention designed to motivate college aspirations could be judged a failure if it used one-year test scores as a proxy for other effects and thereby missed the impacts on things like parental involvement or long-term grit—things that are important but harder or more time-consuming to measure.

Like the policy interventions they study, RCTs should be carefully examined themselves. While there will be times when a single multisite RCT will argue convincingly for a major expansion or termination of a policy or program, serious care and examination should be given to judging whether the study itself is airtight and whether the study calls for reforms and improvements (a "scalpel approach") as opposed to termination.

We must also ensure that RCTs do not become a vehicle to question the underlying mission or need for government to address inequality and opportunity for young people and their families. In research labs across the country, high standards and peer review are used to judge experiments. When trial lab experiments fail, the data are used to guide future experiments and to better understand the science—not as rationales for giving up on collective efforts to, say, find cures for cancer. That same principle should apply to the nation's most stubborn social and economic challenges. RCTs should be used to better inform the right policies to cure major social and economic ills, not as excuses to abandon the mission.

CONTINUUM IN ACTION: COLLEGE OPPORTUNITY

An area that illustrates the need for this kind of approach is college opportunity—helping make sure disadvantaged kids can get to and graduate from college.[19]

We know from rigorous evaluations that a completed college degree has a big impact on economic mobility. Low-income youth experience distressingly little economic mobility in general. For example, a child born to parents in the lowest income quintile has a 42 percent chance of remaining stuck there and a two-thirds chance of ending up in the bottom 40 percent simply due to the accident of birth. But studies show that one surefire way to increase economic mobility for low-income youth is promoting college completion.

When a young person born in the lowest quintile graduates from college, she has an 84 percent chance of moving out of that quintile and as good of a chance of getting to the top quintile as staying in the bottom.[20]

There has also recently been an impressive spate of rigorous data that shows that even high-achieving, low-income youth often do not go to the colleges that fit their abilities. Just 8 percent of these low-income achievers apply to colleges in the strategic way that is recommended for their high-income peers (like sending applications to safety, peer, and reach schools).[21] This results in such students "undermatching"—that is, attending schools below their academic level.

There have been excellent studies showing that relatively low-cost interventions can make a difference. For example, allowing students to send their ACT scores for free to four colleges rather than three might not seem like a big intervention, especially when you consider that a fourth report costs a student just six dollars. Yet, when ACT Inc. made this change, students applied to more colleges and low-income students started attending more selective ones.[22] In addition, providing high-achieving, low-income students with information on the college-application process and with application-fee waivers, again at a cost of just six dollars per student, has been shown to increase the likelihood of college matching by an astounding 31 percent.[23]

There are many other low-cost interventions that could success fully address the problem. Sometimes graduating seniors intend to enroll in college but for a variety of reasons, including missing deadlines, fail to matriculate. Research shows that simply texting students and parents reminders about the matriculation process can substantially reduce this phenomenon, known as "summer melt."[24] While none of these interventions will single-handedly solve the college opportunity problem, they each show that low-cost actions can produce meaningful results and have the most rigorous academic evidence to support their findings.

Still, many of the high-rigor evaluations in the area of college opportunity are geared toward the existing pool of already high-achieving low-income students. If we limit policy interventions to this area alone, we will miss critical interventions aimed at more disadvantaged and vulnerable students at younger ages, which can impact whether they even make it into the group of college-ready, low-income youth. We need to expand the pool—and that requires looking beyond those programs that have already been subject to the most rigorous evidence and investing in promising interventions that have yet to be more rigorously studied.

At this stage, there are intensive efforts for such students that show promise. Studies suggest, for example, that enrolling low-income students in programs that provide mentors, college summer visits, near-peer mentoring, advice on courses, and SAT or ACT prep can meaningfully improve outcomes. Nonprofit or government programs, such as College Track, Posse, I Have a Dream, National College Advising Corps, and Project GRAD, as well as federal programs such as GEAR UP, may well increase the pool of young people with the expectations, know-how, and tools to reach college and succeed there—as long as the programs are intensive and stay with the young people for years.[25] This is an area where there are many case studies and data on outcomes but where there is too often a lack of the most rigorous RCTs to determine which elements of the interventions are most (and least) critical to success. Yet these young people can't put their lives on hold while new ten-year RCTs on college early interventions are launched. In cases like this, the most prudent course must be to utilize the best evidence possible in the near term while tying any significant future expansion to the requirement of more exacting analysis in the long term.

BETTER MEASUREMENTS

As we move toward more rigorous evaluation, we must also undertake the challenge of improving the measurement tools we use to figure out whether a policy is working. Simply put, if we aren't counting the right things, we can't come to the correct conclusions. This is no doubt a subject for a broader conversation and a book unto itself. But one example, in particular, is quite informative on the matter: the case of the poverty measure and what it tells us about tax credits designed to reduce poverty.

When the fiftieth anniversary of the War on Poverty was commemorated in 2014, there was much debate over the degree of poverty reduction America has experienced since President Johnson's ambitious effort. But that debate was dramatically hampered by several flaws in the official poverty measure, whose design did not count many of the major antipoverty efforts that had been implemented over the past fifty years.

Indeed, long before this anniversary, experts across the political spectrum recognized that the official poverty measure, in use for decades, was not ideal. Most critically, it focuses on before-tax cash income, meaning that many policies to combat poverty are not measured. For example, food stamps, housing assistance, the Earned Income Tax Credit (EITC), and the Child Tax Credit are not taken into account when determining a family's resources. The official measure also does not factor in health insurance premiums or out-of-pocket medical expenses, in addition to several other drawbacks.[26]

Over the past five years, policy makers have created the Supplemental Poverty Measure (SPM), which attempts to address many of these problems.[27] The SPM includes the impact of refundable tax relief, or what I call "equal-value tax credits." With the improved SPM, we not only get a better sense of poverty trends, but we also have better data with which to assess the effects of policies. Evidence that the impact of specific policies can alter the incidence of poverty or affect economic mobility are powerful reminders that much about these trends is within our control and can be changed today—for better or worse. Using a more accurate poverty measure has helped us conclude that these tax credits—particularly the EITC—play a substantial role in reducing poverty in America.

EVIDENCE OF REDUCING POVERTY

While the SPM includes data going back to 2009, researchers at Columbia have worked on extending it back further,[28] and experts at the Center on Budget and Policy Priorities (CBPP) have successfully been able to devise a methodology that, while not as complete as the SPM, goes back fifty years and allows rough estimates of how increases in the EITC and other refundable tax credits have affected poverty.[29] The difference in poverty reduction is startling. The Columbia researchers show with their construction of a historical SPM that the poverty rate would have *risen* by six percentage points from 1967 to 2012 in the absence of government benefits, but instead the rate *fell* by three percentage points, a nine-point swing.[30] And focusing specifically on refundable tax credits and the Supplemental Nutrition Assistance Program (SNAP), CBPP estimates that poverty fell eight percentage points from 1964 to 2011, twice the reduction suggested by the official poverty measure.

Much has happened since 1993, when, according to the new method, the EITC moved 1.6 million Americans above the poverty threshold.[31] That year there was a dramatic expansion of the EITC for families with two or more children. In 1997, families on the EITC were allowed to utilize the newly established Child Tax Credit before the EITC when figuring their taxes, which led to another large increase in the amounts going to millions of EITC families.[32] That same year, the new Child Tax Credit also included a small degree of refundability for families with three children or more, which set an important precedent for future reform. Indeed, in 2001, the refundability of the Child Tax Credit, begun in 1997, was dramatically expanded.[33] Finally, in 2009, President Obama signed another expansion—reducing the marriage penalty for EITC couples, increasing benefits for those with three children or more,[34] and allowing the college tax credits started in 1997 to be partially refundable for the first time.[35]

As a result, the SPM and CBPP calculations show that the number of families moved out of poverty by the combined weight of the EITC and Child Tax Credit grew to more than 10 million. The number of children moved out of poverty by these interventions now totals more than 5 million. Moreover, of the 10 million Americans who avoided poverty, fully 1.5 million escaped because of the 2009 expansion in credits.[36]

It's important to note that the actual impact of policies like the EITC could be better or worse depending on the behavioral impacts of the EITC. Neither the new nor the official poverty measures include the behavioral impacts of the policies they count in their calculations. While researchers at CBPP and Columbia have sought to compare the poverty rate counting cash transfers and the rate not counting cash transfers, they aren't actually able to show precisely what the poverty rate would be in the absence of the transfer program in the way that an RCT or quasi-experimental analysis could. In Glenn's terms, they have not directly tested the counterfactual. If the introduction of the EITC had reduced work effort—which the vast bulk of evidence does not support—then the method used by

CBPP might overstate the EITC's impacts on poverty because it would be the case that without the EITC, people would work more and experience less poverty.

However, we now have a good number of careful quasi-experimental studies showing that the EITC *increases* work levels. For example, a 2001 study found that of the 8.7 percentage point increase in the annual employment of single mothers from 1984 to 1996, 61 percent was due to the EITC.[37] Nada Eissa and Jeffrey Liebman found that the expansion of the EITC in 1986 increased the participation rate of single mothers by 2.8 percent compared to those without children,[38] and a recent paper by Bruce Meyer found that the 2009 expansion could increase employment of single mothers with at least three children by 3.7 percent.[39] As for reducing hours worked, studies have shown that the impact is likely small. Single mothers already working do not appear to reduce their hours as a result of the EITC.[40] There is little evidence that the phaseout rates have a big impact on worker behavior, in part because the rate schedule is rather complicated and likely understood by few recipients.[41] Thus, the behavioral impacts of the EITC seem to be clearly on the net-positive side. Based on this research, there is strong reason to believe that CBPP's method, if anything, *understates* the impact of the EITC on reducing poverty.

EVIDENCE OF STABILIZING POVERTY IN RECESSIONS

The data also reveal that equal-value tax credits play a critical role in serving as automatic poverty stabilizers during recessions.

In 2011, when the economy was two years out of our nation's worst downturn since the Great Depression, the official poverty rate was 15 percent. While this is far above the 12.5 percent rate in 2007, it could be argued that it was at least consistent with the 15.1 percent poverty rate that existed in 1993 after a relatively typical recession.[42]

Yet, when we look at the SPM, we see something far more striking. According to CBPP's calculations, the poverty rate in 1993 was 13 percent. And with a full counting of the increased policies since 1993—particularly the increase in the EITC and the refundable Child Tax Credit—the poverty rate in 2011 was 10.9 percent. The improved measurement tool thus offers an important insight: the expansions of equal-value tax credits—together with the expansion of food stamps—have played a major role in economic stabilization for individuals and their families. It is no small feat that due to expansions in these programs, the poverty rate could be two full points lower after the most devastating downturn since the Great Depression than it was roughly the same amount of time after an average recession.

THE POWER OF SUCCESS

What should be clear is that whether one is seeking to allocate resources more efficiently in times of scarcity or to make the case for significant expansions in investments to address critical needs, evidence of success is the best assurance for policy makers that they are fulfilling their responsibilities. It also should be clear that, in the absence of perfect evidence, it is still essential that policy makers gather the most useful information available in the short term, as they—and we—move toward an evidence-driven future.

There is great power in evidence and in proving success. It is the power not just to change outcomes but to change minds, to convince policy makers—and the public—that we can move the needle and genuinely improve the lives of our fellow Americans, as well as the poor we seek to empower in other countries. That is a worthy goal whatever your political affiliation or ideology, and it is one we are on the cusp of embracing. It's just a matter of playing Moneyball the right way.

Chapter IV.

MAKING MONEYBALL WORK

By **Melody Barnes**
Director of the White House Domestic Policy Council under
President Barack Obama

John Bridgeland
Director of the White House Domestic Policy Council under
President George W. Bush

I f you were to design a city from scratch, there are some obvious things you'd want your mayor or city manager to know: how often first responders get to the scene on time, how quickly park workers repair vandalism, how often a library patron is looking for a book the library doesn't have. Without that kind of data, it would be hard to know some basic things—like whether you need to hire more paramedics or consider purchasing new books. But with it, you'd know the baseline facts, and thus you'd be able to make smarter decisions about everything you do. From our perspective, this would be a dream town—a town where children go to better schools, the streets are safer, and the parks are clean, a town that anybody would be happy to call home.

For the sake of argument, let's call our dream town Sunnyvale. It's the perfect name.

Except for one thing: the name already exists. So do these same performance objectives. In fact, these metrics were among the more than three hundred that came to define success in the actual Sunnyvale, California, ever since city managers introduced their performance-based budget system in the 1970s.[43]

Twenty years later, *Newsday* summed up the impact of the new budget: "Sunnyvale has managed things with 35 to 40 percent fewer employees than similar cities, no service cuts, no employee layoffs, no tax hikes."[44] A policy maker's dream come true, and exactly what we want to accomplish in cities and states across the nation.

Several cities have begun to adopt different versions of this approach to track and improve everything from homelessness to crime to potholes. They are setting strategic goals, using data to measure progress toward those goals, and making course corrections when progress isn't being made. Baltimore and Philadelphia are leading the way, but other cities are recognizing the power of this approach as well.

But can this be done at the national level?

In fact, for decades, national leaders—both Republicans and Democrats—have taken steps to improve the performance of the federal government, by better tracking the right information and using it to inform government's decision making and management. The last century saw blue-ribbon commissions to strengthen government performance and get better results going all the way back to the 1912 Taft Commission, which recommended an executive budget, as well as the 1937 Brownlow Commission, which recommended ways to improve efficiency through reorganization and better management practices. There were two Hoover Commissions in the 1940s and 1950s to reduce the number of government departments and increase their efficiency. There was the Grace Commission in the 1980s, which reported that one-third of all income taxes were consumed by waste and inefficiency and another third escaped collection altogether. And there were other efforts for reform along the way.

In 1990, John Mercer, himself a former mayor of Sunnyvale, joined the staff of U.S. Senator William Roth (R-DE) with the goal of applying his local principles to a population more than two thousand times larger. Together, he and Senator Roth developed a proposal that would become the Government Performance and Results Act of 1993. Among other things, GPRA's purpose was to set agency-specific goals, measure performance against those goals, and report publicly on progress made (or not made).

As the bill moved through Congress, the man who would eventually sign it into law was running for president. His name appeared on the dust jacket of *Reinventing Government*—a book that featured Sunnyvale's performance-based budgeting. "Those of us who want to revitalize government in the 1990s," then governor Bill Clinton wrote, "have to reinvent it."

Once in office, President Clinton did more than sign and implement GPRA. He also tasked Vice President Gore with leading an initiative that would eventually take the same name as the book Clinton praised in 1992—one intended to expand the use of performance metrics as well as to reform the federal civil-service and procurement processes.

What made GPRA special was that it went further and deeper than any previous effort to build something new into the structure of government: a system to focus federal departments and agencies on results and provide actionable information to executive-branch managers and members of Congress. The Congressional Research Service called GPRA a "watershed" for the federal government. "For the first time, Congress established statutory requirements for most agencies to set goals, measure performance, and submit related plans and reports to Congress."[45]

And yet, after all that important work, why haven't we seen more progress in addressing our nation's great challenges? Despite significant government investments in young people and their families over the years, Americans are still not prepared for the twenty-first-century workforce. American families are still experiencing little social mobility and growing inequality. Why? What's missing?

Part of the answer, we believe, is evidence and evaluation. We often know what problems need to be solved, but that doesn't mean we are making the *right* kinds of investments to address them. In many cases, we still don't know what the right kinds of investments are.

We have government programs that don't work very well but take up precious resources. We have others that work effectively but are dangerously underfunded. And we have many more for which we just don't know whether they are generating good outcomes. This is where the gap between improving performance and improving results lies. Our goal can't just be to do more things better, especially if they are the wrong things. We need to do the right things well.

The consequences of not having this powerful information can be measured in the lives of those it affects. You can see the cost in the single mother seeking out job training who enrolls in a program that doesn't work. She is wasting precious time and doesn't know it. You can see the cost in the children who don't get to enroll in an early-education program—one that we know will change the trajectory of their lives—because there isn't room for any more students.

And so as we consider this new effort, we have to ask ourselves: What was missing from these previous attempts at improving the performance of government? And what can we do differently to make the absolute best use of government investments?

One answer is clear: we need more high-quality evidence about what works to inform our investments, and we need policy makers and elected officials to use that information to make better choices.

We know that social problems are complex, and the things that matter may be difficult to measure. Often, the drivers for community-wide social progress can be difficult to evaluate. We also realize that experts differ on the kind and scope of "evidence" that should matter most, and that large-scale rigorous studies often show that interventions may have marginal or no effect. That leaves policy makers frustrated as they look for clear solutions, and well-intentioned providers fearful of the very idea of evaluation and evidence building.

But that doesn't mean we should walk away from a "what works" approach. We must tackle today's challenges with the best information we have right now, while simultaneously engaging in a vigorous debate. And ultimately, we need to reorient government—at every level—so that evidence matters more in *all* policy and funding decisions. Right now, we're far from an environment where this is true, at any level of government.

The pursuit of better evidence is an idea that was embraced by both President George W. Bush and President Obama. When President Bush was in office, he oversaw the creation of a new Program Assessment Rating Tool that established a system to analyze government programs—everything from design to implementation to results—and used the diagnostic data to guide the administration's budget decisions.[46] When President Obama took office, he expanded funds to evaluate programs in several agencies, developed new programs that determine funding levels based on evidence of success, and worked with Congress to further refine GPRA. Together these efforts represent a great untold story of bipartisanship in Washington—a partnership across presidencies to improve the performance of government and to make it more results oriented.

But these efforts must be scaled and expanded in order for them to be felt government-wide. That's the challenge at the heart of this Moneyball movement.

So how do we do it? We've consulted academics and experts, conferred with former White House colleagues and state and local officials, and spoken to friends with dozens of years of experience in federal departments and agencies and on Capitol Hill. And we've come to believe that the reason evidence-based government isn't more widespread is that the foundation to allow it to work hasn't been built . . . at least not yet. So our goal is actually fairly straightforward. To mix our baseball-movie metaphors, if we build it, better results will come.

How can leaders implement evidence-based programs if the government itself is not designed to seek out evidence or make funding decisions based on this evidence? How can we get better results when evidence of impact simply does not matter much in policy and funding decisions? It can't be done. That's why we must first build a framework within which Moneyball principles can thrive.

Right now, it's like we're playing T-ball in a sandlot. We don't keep score, we don't know what inning it is, but everybody still gets a trophy. What we need is a professional stadium—with the facilities, umpires, and analytical leadership necessary to perform at the highest levels.

This framework boils down to the three principles we've discussed from the very beginning:

1. Build evidence about the practices, policies, and programs that will achieve the most effective and efficient results.

2. Invest limited taxpayer dollars in practices, policies, and programs that use evidence and evaluation to demonstrate that they work.

3. Direct funds away from practices, policies, and programs that consistently fail to achieve measurable outcomes.

With evidence in hand, policy makers can learn more about what interventions are actually effective. They can then use that information to direct funds toward programs that work; to continuously learn, and use that information to improve programs; and to direct funds away from those programs that consistently prove ineffective.

So how do we do that? As you are about to see, the ideas on our to-do list are modest, noncontroversial, and, even in today's political environment, achievable. In a Washington where there is often the will but simply no way, we find ourselves in an opposite situation. There's a clear way to get this done; we just need the will to do it.

AN ABSENCE OF EVIDENCE

As many current members of Congress, cabinet secretaries, and other policy makers know, if you want to see evidence of impact, chances are you're not just going to be disappointed; you're going to be completely shocked. For the amount of money we spend on social goals we generally support, we often know next to nothing about whether what we're doing is really working, or how.

There are few areas where this is more frustrating than around job training. Though Democrats and Republicans have widely differing views on how best to promote job creation in the United States, there are very few people, elected or otherwise, who would reject the notion that, as the global economy continues to transform, American workers looking for jobs are going to need to develop new skills. Laid-off autoworkers in Michigan are going to need to learn how to manufacture things like high-tech batteries. Struggling coal miners in West Virginia are going to need to learn how to earn a living extracting natural gas instead.

It is, then, not at all surprising that a touchstone of our bipartisan economic strategy has been job-training programs. In the last two decades, we have spent hundreds of billions of dollars on programs to help people develop the skills they need for employment. We've trained hundreds of thousands of people in one form or another.

And yet we have very little sense of how well those programs work—or if they work at all. A report by the Government Accountability Office (GAO) in 2011 highlighted that while the federal government spent $18 billion on forty-seven different job programs, "little is known about the effectiveness of most programs."[47]

Why is that the case? For one thing, responsibilities are split between two sets of programs—job training and student loans — and the entities in charge don't work well together. But more importantly, we are not even collecting some of the most basic data. We don't have good information on how many people who use taxpayer money for job training actually get a degree or occupational credential. And we have terrible information on how many people get jobs related to their training. According to the GAO, states didn't know the types of jobs attained by *more than half* the participants in adult job training.[48]

Can you imagine? This isn't a complex randomized controlled trial to determine if the effects of the program are being caused by other factors. This is figuring out what people who finished job training are doing now!

And let's not forget, securing jobs for the unemployed is not a small-scale economic side project; it's one of our central projects, an unquestionably crucial precursor to the kind of shared economic prosperity each of us, regardless of party, is seeking. In 2014, Congress rewrote the major job-training programs in a way that will streamline the number of programs and improve accountability. But, even with these solid improvements, we still have a long way to go.

And this is just one example. Imagine the list of things we need to know—really need to know—that we can't figure out because we don't even bother to collect the information that would tell us.

Then there are times when, thankfully, we do venture to collect data, but frustratingly, it's not the data we need. Other times, we collect the right data, but we don't create a mechanism to share them across government programs or agencies. That means that there are countless providers who are being required to report the same thing, in slightly different formats to different agencies, creating a big waste and burden for the provider and a patchwork of data that is not easily integrated.

We all have the desire to make government investments more effective. But, as you can see, there is a lot of basic infrastructure that needs to be built before we'll know that we are collecting the right information—and so that evidence can be developed and used widely to make decisions. So first things first: we need to build an evidence base.

BUILD EVIDENCE FOR WHAT WORKS

START WITH THE 1 PERCENT SOLUTION.

Dedicating 1 percent of the existing budget for every federal department and agency to evaluate the effectiveness of its programs could produce a dramatic return on investment. The information gathered by this 1 percent investment can drive—in a more high-impact direction—the other 99 percent of dollars that an agency spends.

Without the evidence, we'll keep missing essential information about programs that aren't working and—just as important—ones that are. Take, for example, the Youth Opportunity Grants program from the late 1990s, which got the axe in 2004 before the program had been sufficiently evaluated. It wasn't until years later that the U.S. Department of Labor finally studied the defunct program and found that Youth Opportunity Grants had reduced the number of out-of-school youth, boosted employment rates, and increased hourly wages in key groups that had been struggling.

DEVELOP AND USE RAPID, LOW-COST TOOLS TO DETERMINE IMPACT.

Having an evidence base and using it wisely means having power—the power to double down confidently on a program that's working or to change course on one that is not. In some cases, it allows us to do more than just understand whether a program works; it allows us to make real-time program improvements to an intervention, at a very low cost. Government needs to get curious—and have the data to learn over time.

Where possible, governments should develop and use rapid, low-cost evaluation tools, like the kinds Glenn and Gene referenced in their chapters. In his thought-provoking book *Uncontrolled: The Surprising Payoff of Trial-and-Error for Business, Politics, and Society*, Jim Manzi describes the ways that leading companies have been using technology to lower the cost of conducting randomized experiments and to determine which approach to a problem will be most effective and why.[49] While we recognize that many challenges facing children and families are significantly more complicated than, for instance, a product-placement question being faced by a retail company, we think there is great promise with these kinds of low-cost tools. And we feel strongly that governments at all levels should explore how to use these tools to improve results.

For example, a government could make a slight tweak to the way a service is provided to one subsection of participants and then compare the outcomes with the other. As a paper Scott Cody and Andrew Asher wrote for the Hamilton Project explains, the New York Human Resources Administration was interested in solving an acute problem: too many children receiving cash assistance from the government were not receiving child support from their non-custodial parent.[50] They hypothesized that one of the reasons for the low rate was that noncustodial parents were required to make a court appearance to establish support. What if they changed the procedures so that the court appearance was no longer required?

Rather than run a complex randomized experiment over a number of years, they could have their answer in a number of months at minimal cost. They simply changed the procedure for a random sampling of noncustodial parents—no more court!—and then watched to see if an uptick in child support followed. What they found was that there was essentially no difference at all in terms of how many parents established child support (57.3 percent versus 56.5 percent for the control group).

Too often in government, we come across a hypothesis that feels like it makes sense and instead of testing it, we assume it will work. We say, as New York could have in this instance, "Court appearances seem like they're the problem, so getting rid of them will be our solution." Then we move on, feeling like we've made progress, without ever knowing if we did.

Had these New York administrators gone that route, they would probably be deploying those new procedures today. But instead they ran tests and figured out that eliminating court appearances would not be beneficial. By conducting this rapid, low-cost experiment, New York City saved itself a new headache and was able to dedicate itself to testing more effective solutions.

CREATE "WHAT WORKS CLEARINGHOUSES" ACROSS GOVERNMENT.

That New York now has this information is great. But it also raises another important question: How do the rest of us get access to information about what works? How can we make sure that other administrators, other program providers, and other policy makers and elected officials at all levels of government have access to the best information that already exists without having to repeat experiments or have them perform their own time-consuming scans?

The bottom line is, for Moneyball to work, we need a way to share the evidence we gather. It needs to be available—and understandable—online, so that it can be understood when read by a policy maker or a program provider. This matters not just so that we can have access to good information but also so we can be confident that bad results aren't being hidden.

Today in some departments, this problem is being addressed with what's known as What Works Clearinghouses (WWC), which operate at the intersection between building the evidence base and making the decision to put funds to their most effective use. It's been done before to good effect. The U.S. Department of Education established a What Works Clearinghouse in 2002 to identify studies that "provide credible and reliable evidence of the effectiveness of a given practice, program, or policy." This office critically surveys existing scientific literature and assesses the evidence. It also conducts thorough reviews of current programs. The Department of Labor established its own clearinghouse in 2014.

Building a federal government-wide What Works Clearinghouses will help government take a hard look in the mirror, and building the evidence base will be like defogging the glass. We should have such clearinghouses across departments and agencies of government.

INVESTING IN WHAT WORKS AND DIRECTING FUNDS AWAY FROM WHAT DOESN'T

As our evidence base grows more robust, policy makers and administrators will inevitably increase their confidence in funding what works. They will also adjust and improve promising programs as they learn valuable lessons over time. And in some cases, they will use evidence to shift resources away from those programs that are proven to be consistently ineffective over time.

A MONEYBALL INDEX

The simple act of requesting and considering evidence as part of the congressional committee process has the potential to improve accountability in lawmaking and administration. Access to environmental-impact statements has allowed Congress to protect Americans from water and air pollution. Access to data about the degree to which legislation imposed an unfunded mandate on local and state governments has led to sponsors of legislation adjusting their bills or reducing their costs.[31] While budget deficits are a real issue, you can be sure they would be a lot worse if the Congressional Budget Office (CBO) did not tell Congress how much every new bill is going to cost the taxpayer. And this shouldn't surprise us. Congress can make far more informed judgments by having access to the right information at the right time. We need more where this came from. We need new proposals and reauthorizations to be considered against a "Moneyball Index."

A Moneyball Index would require sponsors and committees, in the context of new legislation and reauthorizations, to highlight what evidence—if any—exists for a given program and what we have learned about the effectiveness of similar programs over time. Where possible, the index would also include a comparison between the costs of a program and its likely benefits, to see if spending is really worth it.

It would prompt a sponsor to summon the evaluations and evidence that currently exist to show that a particular program demonstrated impact before legislation was drafted. Appropriators could routinely request evaluations from federal departments and agencies, universities, nonprofit programs, researchers, and think tanks on various programs they fund. Evaluations would have to be transparent and give policy makers information about how rigorous the analysis was—a randomized controlled trial, survey data, or something in between.

In cases where members see that little or no evidence exists, they should be prompted to invest in better data gathering and evaluations that will build the evidence that matters, and then direct the federal agency or department's What Works Clearinghouse to make this publicly available. In cases where strong evidence shows that a program is producing outcomes, such efforts could be scaled. Finally, in cases where the evidence is clear that the program is not producing outcomes, authorizers could eliminate or reshape programs, and appropriators could save taxpayers money or reinvest in efforts that are effective. With this proper foundation, government could play Moneyball.

CONTINUOUSLY REVIEW, LEARN, AND INNOVATE

Done right, Moneyball can become an extraordinary tool for delivering better outcomes across the board. But done wrong, there is some risk that it could become a bludgeon, killing programs indiscriminately (the "on-off switch" Gene describes in his chapter). Programs that are consistently shown not to work should be improved or eliminated because they are not serving populations in need and are wasting precious taxpayer money. At the same time, such populations should not be left without alternatives that can help them climb the ladder of opportunity and become self-sufficient.

Moneyball isn't a process by which we should blindly sort through a pile of data and evidence, putting programs into two piles: keep or kill. It is, instead, about using data and evidence as tools to make better, more informed decisions and help improve all programs. There will always be judgment calls (as well as political calls!) that inform choices. But Moneyball will help us to identify interventions that are *more* effective and bring them efficiently to scale to reach more of those in need; it's about learning from practices, policies, and programs along the way so that successful components can be scaled and ineffective components pared away.

And yes, it is also about improving or defunding programs that are proven to be ineffective.

One possible way to prevent the misuse of Moneyball—either through the politicization of evidence or the use of less-than-rigorous studies as a justification for cuts in services—is to identify an impartial referee to evaluate studies and data that come through the door, whether that be a nonpartisan office like CBO or a newly created one.

In the meantime, we ought to embrace innovation and experimentation as much as possible. No one has a monopoly on the right ideas, and that certainly includes us. When it comes to creating the conditions where Moneyball can work, there are many good ideas—big and small.

That's why our final recommendation is that we continue to innovate. There are lots of smart and creative ways to build evidence. We know, because we're already seeing them in action.

In recent years, government has begun to create programs that link levels of funding to levels of evidence—like the Investing in Innovation Fund (i3) at the U.S. Department of Education—so that the more evidence of effectiveness you have, the more money you can get. But that's not all: these programs also say that evaluations will be conducted along the way so that we're always learning from what we are doing.

Another approach—called Pay for Success—goes a step further. It pays private and nonprofit service providers not when they *promise* success but after they actually *deliver* success. These "social-impact bonds" create incentives for risk-averse governments to try a promising new approach, and create powerful incentives for partners to deliver better outcomes at lower costs.[52]

Before the program commences, all parties agree on the outcomes to be achieved and the measurement methodology they'll use to demonstrate success or failure. This model was pioneered in the United Kingdom, where in 2010, the City of Peterborough used it to focus on reducing recidivism among short-term offenders. It did so—to the tune of a 10 percent reduction. New York City is also experimenting with Pay for Success. In 2012, the city implemented the first social-impact bond in the United States in the Rikers Island jail with investment funding from Goldman Sachs and the Bloomberg Family Foundation. The investment funds the largest-scale implementation ever of an evidence-based cognitive-behavior-therapy program designed to reduce recidivism for those aged 16–18 by at least 10 percent over two years. Preliminary results will be available in late 2015.

Pay for Success is among a number of exciting new ideas that are already helping us do more of what works. There are challenges to work out—such as how to ensure that programs don't focus on the easiest to serve and push out the hardest to serve, and how to measure and account for savings that might occur at multiple levels of government but might be realized only at one level of government. (For example, if a city increases access to early-childhood education, special education or health-care resources may be saved at the state or federal level rather than at the city level.) From our perspective, there's only more innovation to come.

We also have the opportunity, as we learn, to adapt. Some of the things we try won't work, or they will but will need to be tweaked. We should be open to doing so. For instance, the Department of Education's What Works Clearinghouses have been important steps forward, but in their early implementation we've learned that we need to do a better job of disseminating information gained from them, and that we need to be gathering a broader range of evidence that can be used by policy makers and practitioners who need to act today, while more rigorous studies are being conducted.

What we find most exciting about this list of priorities is what *isn't* on it. We don't need complicated new legislation or big new spending. Nothing will require a constitutional amendment or a court fight. We don't even have to wait for the current, toxic political environment to shift (more on that in the next chapter).

Instead, we can take a number of relatively modest steps that will dramatically improve the data and evidence that policy makers and elected officials have access to in order to make better decisions. In this way, a relatively unexciting but achievable list can get us to a very exciting and ambitious place—a place where we can have the evidence to make a bold proclamation ("Solve ten social problems in the next ten years!") and feel more confident that we know the best way to follow through. For those of us who have worked with these issues for years, these achievable changes in process add up to one big reason we're so optimistic about playing Moneyball for government.

Chapter V.

EMBRACING THE POLITICS OF MONEYBALL

By **Kevin Madden**
Republican political strategist

Howard Wolfson
Democratic political strategist

This is not the first time a bipartisan group of serious thinkers has come together to propose an important new idea. And let's be honest: not many of those attempts have actually changed the way we do things in Washington. There are any number of reasons for that, not least of which is the contentious political environment where these ideas have been introduced. Today, of course, is no exception, and we wouldn't be surprised if some of you reading this right now have concluded that Moneyball for government is a great idea but still wonder if it ever really has a chance of being put into action.

Fortunately, while it's true that there are very real obstacles to making Moneyball work, it's also true that there's a clear path forward on both sides of the aisle. Democrats and Republicans may fight like cats and dogs—feral ones at times—but the Moneyball approach offers a lot for both sides to like and to capitalize on. Case in point: the two of us are advocating for it together from a political perspective, a space where we almost never agree with each other. After all, Howard is a former executive director of the Democratic Congressional Campaign Committee. He was a senior adviser on Hillary Clinton's 2008 presidential campaign—and on both of her Senate campaigns—before becoming a deputy mayor of New York City in Mayor Michael Bloomberg's data-driven administration. Kevin was also on the campaign trail in 2008, advising Mitt Romney—a role he reprised in 2012 as Governor Romney's spokesman and senior strategist. We have sparred privately and publicly on a range of issues on any number of occasions. But on this one, we both agree: government should—and can—play Moneyball.

In this chapter, we'll do a couple of things: First, we'll explain why we think the political environment in general is ripe for a Moneyball movement. Then, we'll each draw on our experiences as political strategists to outline the different obstacles Moneyball will face, and offer our advice about how to overcome them. Kevin will speak to the Republican Party's unique circumstances, and then Howard will explain things on the other side of the aisle.

THE POLITICAL ENVIRONMENT IS BETTER THAN YOU THINK

During the 2012 presidential election, a full 15 percent of voters surveyed said that the federal budget deficit was the most important issue facing the country. That was three times the number who cited foreign policy as their top concern and only narrowly behind those who named health care. Leading up to the 2014 midterm elections, 80 percent of respondents in a Gallup poll indicated that they worried about the federal budget deficit a great deal or a fair amount. And it's no wonder they worry. An April 2014 Reason-Rupe poll revealed that Americans believe the problem is far worse than it is; a majority estimated that the government wastes as much as fifty cents of every taxpayer dollar received. There's no question: how to spend government revenue more effectively is very much on the minds of the American people, Democrats, and Republicans.

Yet while nearly 90 percent of Americans say they want the federal government to devote "a lot or a great deal of effort" to solving the country's budget challenges, 85 percent doubt that DC is capable of doing so. Their skepticism is well founded, as our budgeting process has completely broken down. Congress has met the deadline for passing a budget on time only once since 1997. More often than not, Congress doesn't even *pass* a budget, preferring instead to put forward pie-in-the-sky documents that energize political bases and have no chance of actually being enacted into law. The past few years of debt-ceiling standoffs, midnight "fiscal cliffs," and a government shutdown have meant that—far from thoughtfully considering how we're spending taxpayer dollars—we lurch from crisis to crisis, stopgap to stopgap, kicking the can still farther down the road. This is a problem for both parties; if that skepticism hardens, many members of Congress can expect to lose their jobs.

In that sense, Moneyball represents an opportunity—and an important one at that—for Democrats and Republicans to work together in a serious, thoughtful, and measured way without forcing either side to step on political land mines. But *opportunity* does not mean *guarantee*. There will still be obstacles for both political parties and some degree of tentativeness on the part of skeptical officials. But we believe these challenges can be overcome.

From here, Kevin will walk you through the biggest obstacle on the Republican side, and then Howard will take over on Democrats.

good article

KEVIN FOR THE REPUBLICANS:
FROM ANTIGOVERNMENT TO EFFICIENT GOVERNMENT

When I talk to people who aren't very familiar with the idea of evidence-based policy making, I find myself entertaining the same question over and over again: But what about the Tea Party? They'd never go for this, would they?

This skepticism grows out of a common view among Republicans—within and beyond the establishment—that the Tea Party, and by extension the Republican base, is reflexively antigovernment. Not just in some cases, but in all cases. And because the party establishment has had a string of primary losses, including former U.S. House majority leader Eric Cantor's stunning loss in 2014, Republicans continue to pay special attention to what the base thinks when determining the agenda and ideological positioning of the party. As it should be.

But here's the rub: Republicans are right to listen to the base, to recognize its power, to stop assuming that incumbency is still an advantage. The problem is, they aren't really listening to the base as a whole—just to its loudest voices. In doing so, they risk drawing conclusions about a range of policies, including the Moneyball agenda, that are, frankly, incorrect.

The biggest barrier to overcome on the right is this conventional wisdom—the kind that says that the Tea Party stands against government of all kinds rather than for a smaller, more effective, more accountable government. We have to convince the Republican establishment to take a closer look.

It is a severe misdiagnosis of the Tea Party's recent influence to conclude that it is simply *antigovernment*. Instead, there is a large swath of voters opposed to *inefficient* government, *wasteful* government, and *unaccountable* government. This group of voters represents a reform element inside a center-right electorate that emerges in cycles, animated about taxes, spending, deficits, and a government that is increasingly—they believe—unaccountable to the concerns of ordinary Americans. Their concerns are valid—quite often provable—and they deserve to be heard. But it is an oversimplification to write off as wide-eyed antigovernment fanatics everyone who believes government could function more efficiently and accountably.

For instance, at the height of the 2010 Tea Party wave, a majority of the Tea Party—52 percent—said that they believed the taxes they paid were fair.[53] While more than 90 percent of the Tea Party prefers smaller government,[54] a 2012 CBS poll found that 62 percent of self-identified Tea Party supporters consider government programs such as Social Security and Medicare "worth the costs to taxpayers."[55] In short, conservatives don't want handouts and bloated bureaucracy, but neither do they want to throw the baby (or Social Security) out with the bathwater.

Nuanced analysis reveals that Republicans have a great deal to gain by focusing their political messaging—and policy agenda—on "efficient government" rather than on being "antigovernment." It's a position that lines up with what the majority of the base is seeking and with what a majority of the American people are, too.

A 2013 Pew survey, for example, found that 56 percent of Americans and 87 percent of Republicans prefer "a smaller government providing fewer services." Yet the same study found that fewer than one in five Republicans wants to decrease spending on Medicare or infrastructure. Nearly half of Republicans actually support *increasing* spending on education. Another study found that a majority of Republicans prefer improving government efficiency and performance to merely reducing its size. This is a more nuanced picture than most in the media—and frankly, many in my party—are willing to accept. But it could also be our greatest opportunity.

Instead of framing our message as antigovernment, the GOP should talk about keeping programs in place that work as intended and having the courage to cut those that don't. Republicans should demand high-quality evidence before any new program is created, and Republicans should insist that all discretionary spending be subject to evaluation to determine whether it is having an impact. This would be a powerful—and widely popular—campaign promise. Republicans who support the Moneyball campaign can then run on having the bravery to make the tough decisions to defund or discontinue programs that aren't working or haven't met standards or don't demonstrate positive trends toward success. We should be the party of thrift *and* thoughtfulness, economy *and* empathy, metrics *and* heart. Doing so will give us a smaller government and a bigger tent. It will make our country and our party more competitive. In other words, on both the politics and the policy, Moneyball is a home run—and a no-brainer—for the Republican Party.

Take it from Ronald Reagan, who declared as he accepted the Republican nomination in 1980, "I pledge to you to restore to the federal government the capacity to do the people's work without dominating their lives. I pledge to you a government that will not only work well but wisely, its ability to act tempered by prudence, and its willingness to do good balanced by the knowledge that government is never more dangerous than when our desire to have it help us blinds us to its great power to harm us."[56] If Republicans embrace data, evidence, and evaluation in our policy making, it is within our power to fulfill that pledge today and to create a federal government that will not only work well but wisely.

HOWARD FOR THE DEMOCRATS: DEFINING AND PROTECTING SUCCESS

Poorly written & defensive

During the forty years in the nineteenth century that Charles William Eliot was the president of Harvard University, baseball continued to grow in popularity around the United States. But despite it increasingly becoming the nation's pastime, Eliot was no fan of the game. One year, after Harvard's baseball team finished a successful season, Eliot actually announced that he was considering dropping the sport from the Harvard athletic department. When asked for an explanation, Eliot explained. "Well, this year, I'm told the team did well because one pitcher had a fine curve ball. I understand that a curve ball is thrown with the deliberate attempt to deceive. Surely that is not an ability we should want to foster at Harvard."

You might be asking yourself, "What does any of this have to do with evidence-based government?" Well, Democrats' biggest political risk—and thus the biggest progressive obstacle to implementing evidence-based policy making—is that they are being thrown a Republican curve ball. Democrats justifiably fear that a focus on government efficiency and effectiveness could become a "deliberate attempt to deceive," a way of cutting or eliminating programs that are so critical to opening opportunity and improving lives.

But, the truth is, Democrats have long been strong proponents of improving the way government works. President Clinton and Vice President Gore led a "Reinventing Government" movement in the 1990s. Elected Democrats across the country—from Philadelphia mayor Michael Nutter and Atlanta mayor Kasim Reed to Rhode Island state treasurer Gina Raimondo—are using data and evidence to make tough choices and get better results. Democrats care a lot about making sure that government delivers for all Americans.

At the same time, Democrats have a strong record of fiscal responsibility. President Clinton created America's only budget surplus since the 1960s. President Obama reduced the deficit at the fastest rate since World War II. We aren't squeamish about deficit reduction. We have actually gotten it done, not just talked about it as a priority.

We understand that there has to be a focus both on fiscal responsibility and on how government works and on the critical investments needed to foster growth and opportunity. And the past several years call into question whether Republicans really want to be a partner in that kind of approach. Time and again, they have supported taking a chain saw to the budget rather than a scalpel, hobbling government's ability to deliver for the very people Moneyball is meant to help. A new venture that involves the federal budget could easily be a replay of these past fights, where Republicans use the rhetoric of Moneyball "efficiency" but really mean across-the-board elimination.

This is a challenge. But it is not new. And neither is the Democratic Party's commitment to this fight. We know that this is about more than just dollars and cents; it goes to the core of the values that define what it means to be Democrat.

Democrats care about making people's lives better. We care about lifting people up, about reducing injustice and expanding opportunity. At our core, we are optimists who believe that even the most intractable problems can be solved, and we believe unapologetically that government can play a positive role in solving them.

This is what Moneyball is all about. It's about making sure that we are doing right by the people we've committed ourselves to serving. It's about making sure that our values aren't just articulated in our efforts but in our outcomes, and that we can actually say that we are delivering on our promises.

How can we be willing to marshal the resources to invest in early education but not be willing to make sure we are spending it on the very best preschool?

How can we hold job training up as a solution to our unemployment crisis if we aren't willing to make sure the programs we're funding actually help Americans find work?

Democrats have done so much in this area already. But it's time to do even more. To embrace Moneyball. To own it. To define it not as a debate about the size of our investments but one about investing in what works. Because in the end, making government work well is critical to our entire operating philosophy. It's the idea that government can, in fact, work—that programs aimed at making our health care more affordable, our schools more effective, our economy stronger, and opportunity greater are worth investing in. Among the greatest risks to the progressive agenda is the American people concluding, whether eagerly or reluctantly, that government is not capable of delivering on its promises—that our problems are beyond our capacity to solve. The more people begin to believe that, the more difficult it will be for progressives to get elected and to translate their values into policy.

Consider what happened after the botched rollout of HealthCare.gov. In the months after, public confidence in government plummeted. One *Washington Post* poll showed that 56 percent of Americans believed the website to be part of a more fundamental problem with the law. At the same time, a Pew survey found public trust in government falling to near an all-time low.[57] The same happened after the public learned of the mistreatment of veterans at the VA. A *USA Today* poll found that just one in five Americans thought the government was providing good or excellent care to our veterans. Twice as many felt the same way just three years prior.

This is especially disconcerting when you look at millennials, a generation that powered President Obama's rise to power and will become 40 percent of all eligible voters by 2018. According to a Pew Research Center study, in 2009, 44 percent of millennials thought government does what's right most of the time. By 2013, that "trust rate" dropped to 29 percent. By 2013, 51 percent of millennials said they thought government was inefficient and wasteful.[58] These are the kinds of viewpoints that are far easier to form than they are to change.

Democrats cannot afford to let those opinions solidify. Setting rigorous benchmarks—and then exceeding them—is an incredibly powerful way to rebuild the American people's confidence in the power of government to bring about meaningful change. And rebuilding that confidence may be the most important step the party can take to transform our best ideas into the laws of the land.

Ultimately, I'm confident Democrats will support Moneyball because the payoff it promises is so high for so many of America's most vulnerable citizens. I firmly believe that with a few carefully designed evaluation mechanisms and a lot of hard work and trust, we truly can offer Americans a government that works. That would be good for the country—and good for the party.

KEVIN AND HOWARD: THE COST OF INACTION

In Howard's hometown of New York City, concerned citizens have erected a National Debt Clock by Times Square, tallying the trillions our government spends and how much our excessive spending is costing each American family. There's a similar clock in DC, on Pennsylvania Avenue, about a mile from Kevin's office. The digital display flashes by—tens of thousands of dollars at a time—faster than you can process the numbers. But it's a very big number—and it keeps climbing higher every day.

Meanwhile, in the shadow of those clocks, Americans with no home and no hope sleep on benches. Children walk by who will never get the education they need to succeed. Young people who've made mistakes get caught in the criminal-justice system and stay there. As those clocks keep counting, they mark a deficit well beyond mere financial cost.

So will overcoming these deep-seated political barriers be easy? Hardly. The two of us have spent too much time in the trenches to believe that all of our partisanship will magically disappear. But we've shown that there is a way for the Republican Party to make government work better while also limiting its explosive growth. There is a way Democrats can ensure they won't be conned into dismantling programs that we know can accomplish so much good. There is a way forward. Now it's up to all of us to seize it.

Chapter VI.

FOREIGN ASSISTANCE AND THE REVOLUTION OF RIGOR

By   **Michael Gerson**
Assistant to the President for Policy and Strategic Planning
under George W. Bush

Raj Shah
Administrator of the United States Agency for International
Development under President Obama

When President Kennedy created the U.S. Agency for International Development (USAID) in 1961[59], he did so out of what he described as an inescapable American duty. He talked about our nation's "moral obligations as a wise leader and good neighbor in the interdependent community of free nations." He spoke of our economic obligations "as the wealthiest people in a world of largely poor people." And he discussed our political obligations, describing foreign assistance as "the single largest counter to the adversaries of freedom."

This was by no means the first global effort to render assistance to nations in systemic crisis. In the preceding decades, America famously provided food assistance to the hungry of postwar Europe and other struggling regions around the world. But with the birth of a federal agency dedicated exclusively to international development, the U.S. had both devised a better way to systematically approach global poverty and secured the weight of the presidency behind the effort.

Foreign assistance was, even at its outset, a generally bipartisan affair. President Nixon worked with his political nemesis—Hubert Humphrey—to reform aid funding and redirect it away from large infrastructure programs and toward smaller, community-level projects in health, education, and food security. And he created the Overseas Private Investment Corporation, which offers financing and insurance to companies that invest in emerging markets. "There is a moral quality in this nation that will not permit us to close our eyes to the want in this world," said Nixon in 1969, "or to remain indifferent when the freedom and security of others are in danger."[60]

In the decades since, international development has generally been a powerful tool for good. During the 1980s, development organizations came together to create a campaign for child survival, one that focused aggressively on immunization and vaccination as ways to dramatically reduce infant and child mortality in the developing world. Because of those efforts, child mortality has been cut in half since 1990, even as the world population grew by more than 2 billion people.[61] In places where results-oriented programs have been implemented, the outcomes have typically been undeniable, humane, and inspiring.

But despite the many worthy victories, the dual mission of foreign assistance became a hindrance over time. American leaders in the Cold War era often saw foreign assistance through the lens of geopolitics—not only as an instrument to improve lives, but as a lever to shift alliances and allegiances, to win hearts and minds, to stave off the expansion of the Soviet Union, and to convince the world that democracy was the only route to shared prosperity.

Entangled in that perspective was a problem that would hobble foreign assistance for decades. Increasingly, success was defined by whether the United States provided assistance rather than by whether that assistance produced meaningful outcomes. Aid dollars were treated more as an instrument of politics than as an instrument of development. Decisions about where to spend money—and on what—were highly politicized. Money was wasted. Opportunities to do great good were missed. And trust was spent.

The lack of measured success—of any real evidence that aid was working—created a backlash that exists to this day. It gave opponents of foreign assistance the ammunition they needed to criticize its efficacy, question its purpose, undermine its budgets, and marginalize its mission. And it gave people working within the foreign assistance community reasons to be deeply frustrated, as high-impact projects would go unfunded while money was squandered halfway around the world.

This approach to assistance is no longer adequate, if it ever was. We, the authors, worked in federal government—Michael served as a senior policy adviser and director of speechwriting for President George W. Bush, and Raj served as administrator of USAID for more than five years under President Barack Obama—at a time when foreign assistance efforts have been required to show more rigor, innovation, and professionalism than ever before. When the AIDS pandemic threatened the stability and future of entire nations, and when the Ebola virus emerged from the border region of Guinea to cause a global health emergency, it became immediately clear that effective foreign aid is not simply a geopolitical chess piece. It must serve essential purposes in its own right. And both of us were fortunate to serve presidents who shared and acted on this view.

Despite our differences on a range of ideological issues, our experience has led us to some shared convictions. We believe foreign assistance should be measured in lives changed, not dollars distributed. We believe making friends with other countries should be the by-product of a really good aid program rather than the mission itself. And we believe evidence and data should drive policy and practice. In different roles, in different administrations, we have been part of a revolution of rigor in foreign assistance—incomplete but holding vast promise. And seizing that promise will advance the values and interests of America.

DATA AND EVIDENCE AT WORK

A number of factors have driven this shift toward results-oriented foreign assistance. They include the rise of new, non-institutional philanthropic actors, like the Gates Foundation, which have embraced rigor and evidence as the essential prerequisites of their grant-making efforts. In a field once dominated by large public institutions, there are now more players, including a new generation of evidence-obsessed social entrepreneurs. We've seen such organizations implement their own international programs—for example, Evidence Action and its Deworm the World Initiative, which treated more than 90 million children in a single school year in India and Kenya.[62]

At the same time, there has been a transformational shift among multinational corporations, whose leaders are increasingly looking to nurture emerging markets while proving themselves genuinely positive members of the community. In 2002, for example, Unilever embarked on what one of its brand managers called "a marketing program with social benefits," an effort by the company to educate Indians about the health benefits of soap.[63] A Nielsen survey found that the program, which reached more than 70 million people in its first two years, led 33 percent more mothers in one city to start washing their hands with soap, and 26 percent more children to start washing their hands before meals—which had a meaningful effect both on health outcomes in India and on Unilever's bottom line.[64] Innovative companies are proving it is possible to do well and to do good at the same time.

In the new era of foreign aid, faith-based institutions also are playing an increasingly important role, leveraging their resources to save lives. Saddleback Church, for example—an evangelical megachurch based in Southern California—has made the case that working through faith-based institutions can be more effective than working through public systems, since religious structures in the developing world are often stronger, more broadly distributed, and better trusted. Saddleback has built an army of volunteers, trained them in disease prevention and basic health, and deployed them in places of need. And the church has bold goals: to provide health care access to 650,000 people in the next three years; to carry out 30,000 home and community visits; and to adopt all of the orphans in Rwanda—a goal Saddleback is nearly halfway to achieving.[65] Faith-based institutions, from large global charities to the storefront outreach of local faith leaders, are sources of help and hope, and irreplaceable partners in the delivery of services.

This combination of corporations, foundations, and religious institutions working together with a shared purpose has had a transformational effect, not only in saving lives but in shifting our aid culture away from geopolitics and toward results.

But perhaps no factor has been more important in bringing about this shift than the demand for and commitment to evidence-based assistance that has been articulated by the presidents we were honored to serve. Rather than arguing for an abstract theory, we had the chance to put our vision into action and to see the results.

Those who talk of foreign aid being thrown down a rathole are very much behind the times. The world is, in fact, experiencing something of a golden age when it comes to ambitious, accountable foreign assistance. Though most Americans don't realize it, recent progress, particularly against infectious disease, has been breathtaking. Malaria, for example, once seemed a cruel, inevitable fact of life in parts of Africa. By stepping up the fight against this disease, however, foreign aid organizations have helped save more than 6 million lives and drive incidence down by nearly 60 percent.[66] Or take tuberculosis—because of better funding and better diagnosis, a staggering 37 million deaths from TB have been prevented.[67] America's role in all these gains has been indispensable.

In the process, American aid institutions—"bureaucracies" to their critics—have become some of the most data-driven, outcome-oriented segments of the U.S. government. Results for America, which publishes an annual "Invest in What Works" index that evaluates federal departments and agencies, scored USAID highest when it came to leveraging evidence in its decision-making. There is, of course, considerable room for improvement. But far from being examples of failure, American aid programs have demonstrated a combination of ambition, innovation, and professionalism that makes them a model for government reform efforts in other areas.

Both of us have witnessed the power of evidence and data to transform foreign aid and save millions of lives. And we've learned some lessons in the process that might aid future administrations. Our objective is not to look backward and evaluate outdated practices in foreign assistance, but to look forward with the conviction that results-oriented aid programs with clear goals, metrics, and milestones can have enormous impact.

A NEW WAY OF THINKING: BEST PRACTICES

What follows is a nonpartisan road map of best practices that can continue to transform the way the United States provides foreign assistance. It encompasses the collective wisdom of conversations we had over the years with each other; with experts in the field; with political leaders, both domestic and international; and with the very people on the ground whose lives we all are trying to change. We recognize how challenging this work is, and how easy it would be to revert to old practices. And so we hope these conclusions, accumulated across two administrations, can not only inform the aid reform process but inspire a generation of leaders to commit to a bold new way of thinking.

1. WE MUST BUILD AND MAINTAIN A STRONG POLITICAL CONSENSUS FOR RESULTS-DRIVEN OUTCOMES.

The humorist P.J. O'Rourke once derided bipartisan consensus as one of the most frightening phrases he could imagine, writing, "It's like when my doctor and my lawyer agree with my wife that I need help."[68] In our national climate of deep political polarization, skepticism can be forgiven. Political consensus seems almost archaeological, a fossilized record of how things once were—and might never be again.

Within the realm of foreign assistance, however, the opposite has proved true. Political parties are moving closer together, not further apart. Consensus on foreign assistance hasn't been the result of compromising principles or core values. On the contrary, it has grown out of a genuine meeting of the minds, a shared understanding of what it takes—and what it will take—to lift the world's poor out of impossibly harsh circumstances. Indeed, our achievements in the past fifteen years were made possible by unprecedented alliances between Democrats and Republicans and between faith-based organizations and development advocates.

Perhaps the most dramatic example of this kind of consensus began when Michael was in the White House, advocating alongside others for the President's Emergency Plan for AIDS Relief (PEPFAR).

At the start of the Bush administration, only about 50,000 of an estimated 30 million people with HIV/AIDS in sub-Saharan Africa were on treatment. Average life expectancy on the continent had decreased by fifteen years. If you visited a South African shanty town in early 2000, you would meet mainly grandparents and grandchildren. Much of the intervening generation had been swept away. Millions were dying at the same time and yet in total isolation, surrounded by the barbed wire of stigma.

It was in this context that President Bush decided to create the largest initiative to fight a single disease in history, making the end of global AIDS one of America's highest national priorities. Michael worked with the president on the 2003 State of the Union Address in which he would announce his intentions. "Seldom has history offered a greater opportunity to do so much for so many," Bush said.

What Bush and his team understood—and fully embraced— was that PEPFAR's success was dependent, first and foremost, on building consensus, both around the goal of eradicating AIDS in Africa and around the means by which it could be achieved. Unexpected alliances between progressive activists and conservative political figures had begun to emerge in the late 1990s on issues such as debt relief and global health—most dramatically modeled by the unlikely partnership of the rock star Bono and the late Senator Jesse Helms, who bonded over the moral imperative to save lives in Africa. Members of the PEPFAR political coalition ranged from Representative Nancy Pelosi, a proud San Francisco liberal, to Representative Henry Hyde, a conservative icon. When Bush pushed to reauthorize PEPFAR in 2005, it was Speaker Pelosi who cleared its procedural advance and, from the well of the House, defended the legislation; it was Senator Joe Biden, chair of the Foreign Relations Committee, who pushed for rapid consideration and passage in the Senate. Few other issues have demonstrated such a strong, genuinely nonpartisan coalition.

President Obama took the baton when he assumed office in 2009. Rather than reflexively reversing course, he recognized PEPFAR as the lifesaving program it was. When he built his own Global Health Initiative, he did so with PEPFAR as a model and as its centerpiece. And he fully embraced the consensus structure that President Bush had created.

The results speak for themselves, as some of the broadest gains in public health ever recorded. By 2014, PEPFAR funding was supporting antiretroviral treatment for nearly 8 million people. It was offering HIV testing and counseling services to more than 14 million pregnant women, resulting in 95 percent of their children being born virus-free.[69] According to a National Institutes of Health (NIH) study, PEPFAR has averted 2.9 million infections and saved nearly 9 million children from being orphaned.[70]

The PEPFAR coalition—including disease activists, faith-based conservatives, and national security leaders—serves as a road map for future coalitions seeking to provide development assistance and foreign aid. In fact, USAID's recent ability to rebuild its staff, hire technical leadership, and create and lead presidential initiatives all manifested during a difficult partisan period in American politics, proving the power of moral leadership across the aisle. At the same time, both political parties must remain aware of the pitfalls that could tear such consensus apart, and must work diligently to avoid them. In our experience, this requires a willingness to keep divisive issues off the table. It would be easy, for example, to derail the PEPFAR coalition by bringing reproductive rights into the conversation. But there are wiser forums for such a debate. When it comes to HIV/AIDS, millions of lives have been saved by avoiding culture war controversy—and many lives could be put at risk by inviting it.

American aid institutions also must be careful to avoid letting the record of a country's government determine our willingness to provide humanitarian and development support to its citizens. In Ethiopia, for example, the late Prime Minister Meles Zenawi had a poor human rights record, one certainly worthy of condemnation, yet that did not prevent foreign aid from pouring into the country throughout his tenure. Nor should it have. The goal of foreign assistance is not to change a government but to change the lives of those living under it. American assistance often appropriately includes support for civil society and democratic process, but it is essential that the U.S. remain pragmatically focused on delivering a results-based aid program while also placing appropriate expectations on partner governments.

In the end, our nation's success in delivering rigorous foreign assistance depends on the constant reminder of our purpose and mission, and on a recognition that partisan polarization on this issue is entirely unnecessary and would be particularly destructive.

As former members of presidential administrations, we see this type of leadership, above all, as a presidential responsibility. It is ultimately up to the president to build and sustain a viable political coalition—especially when such a coalition will almost always require strange bedfellows to work together on common aspirations. This is what leadership on foreign assistance is all about.

2. WE MUST CREATIVELY AND RELENTLESSLY EMPLOY TECHNOLOGY AND INNOVATION TO DRIVE MEASURABLE OUTCOMES AND SAVE LIVES.

In 1944, a young microbiologist—having been rejected by the military when he tried to enlist—found himself working on pesticide development for DuPont in Wilmington, Delaware. He'd been at the chemical plant for two years, and now an improbable offer of employment had come his way. The job would be based in Mexico City, which meant he'd have to leave his pregnant wife and daughter at home. DuPont didn't want him to go and reportedly offered to double his salary. It's hard to know exactly what went through Norman Borlaug's mind when he accepted the offer from the Rockefeller Foundation to assist the Mexican government with its wheat production. Could he possibly have imagined then what the world knows now—that his work would go on to save a billion people from starvation?

Maybe he imagined this type of outcome, but he couldn't have known it with any certainty. Nor could the institutions funding his research be sure it would succeed. And yet they chose to fund it anyway.

If you were to tell the story of the Green Revolution, you might begin it this way. But this story can be applied just as easily to other technologies and industry sectors. In almost every case, a future technological transformation is first conceived when a decision is made to fund basic research. Vaccines have eradicated cruel diseases this way. In 1974, fewer than 5 percent of the world's children were vaccinated against six fatal diseases[71]; today, more than 80 percent are. Transgenic seeds have rescued people from hunger this way. Varieties of new, drought-resistant maize can yield 30 percent more than commercial seeds under drought conditions. America continues to fight AIDS this way and to confront Ebola this way. Indeed, science and technology have been at the heart of our nation's most ambitious efforts to save lives. The world has long depended on the United States to drive these investments, and Americans have long embraced this as our obligation.

And yet in recent years, budget pressures have constrained our federal R&D budget in dangerous ways. That isn't just a national challenge; it's a global one, because no other country would fill the void the United States might leave.

Investment in basic research requires a leap of faith. No one can know what such investments will produce—or whether they'll produce anything at all. We don't know how long it will take, or how hard it will be, to achieve success. In some cases, we don't even know what we're preparing for. But there are things we do know. We know that if we wait until emergency strikes to begin research on some matters—say, pandemic flu vaccines—we may be too late. And we know that if we depend on private markets alone to drive R&D, profitability will always be a prerequisite for innovation. The importance of the federal government's role in encouraging research is hard to overstate.

In the aftermath of 9/11, when fears about a weaponized virus intensified, the federal government increased research efforts on an Ebola vaccine. At the time, Ebola had only ever infected a few hundred people in Africa, meaning private companies had no profit motive to pursue this line of inquiry. But the federal government had a different motive and funded a robust effort to tackle the disease. A dozen years later, when Ebola began ravaging West Africa, researchers were already narrowing in on a delivery mechanism for a vaccine. By 2015, clinical trials of the vaccine in Guinea were shown to be "highly efficacious and safe," preventing the disease in all of the vaccinated patients after the first six days.[72]

One of the most important tools to save lives is investment in basic research. Public grants and public–private partnerships should be well funded and robust. This will require partnerships across government—between development agencies and public research institutions like the NIH. USAID will need to continue its work with major companies, especially in the United States, that are engines of innovation. In fact, wherever possible, development agencies should look to private-sector models and apply these to their assistance efforts.

In recent years, for example, there has been a proliferation across government of programs that support entrepreneurs. When

Raj was at USAID, he created his own version: the Development Innovation Ventures (DIV) program. This initiative, modeled after a venture fund, was designed to support evidence-based businesses that want to commercialize their efforts in poor parts of the world and that have a dual impact: building a viable business and reducing poverty. And each effort the DIV funds has gone through a randomized controlled trial or equivalent.

Whether as part of the DIV program or not, development leaders need to adopt a venture capitalist's posture of constantly searching for the next set of technologies and the next big opportunity to leverage, whether it's longer-lasting AIDS drugs or better molecular diagnostics for pandemics.

At the same time, development leaders need to resist scientifically baseless objections to new technologies whose poverty-fighting power is irrefutable. The use of transgenic crop technologies, or "genetically modified organisms" (GMOs), has become the classic example. In the comparatively wealthy United States, there is little cost attached to a decision not to eat GMOs. But to allow that bias against GMOs to bleed into development work, particularly when there isn't any science to back up this preference, is tantamount to letting people starve based on a hunch. We now have drought-tolerant maize for Africa and salt-tolerant rice for Asia. In places where people go hungry, there is a serious cost to the outright banning of GMOs.

Of course, if we are going to deploy technology and innovation to save lives, and if we are going to rely on data to drive our decisions and shape our strategies, we must also focus on improving the ways we collect data itself. Foreign assistance organizations need better systems to produce better metrics, and a more sophisticated structure to monitor the outcomes of decisions we make. The pursuit of such tools must be as much a priority as the crises they are designed to measure.

3. WE MUST APPOINT PEOPLE TO LEAD INTERNATIONAL DEVELOPMENT EFFORTS WHO BELIEVE IN THE POWER OF DATA AND EVIDENCE.

It's important to remember the context in which the two of us are making these recommendations. Keep in mind that while an evidence-based approach may seem obvious, it remains controversial in many circles of the international development community. Many still view the work of foreign assistance through the lens of politics and diplomacy, and tend to see people who believe otherwise as naïve. It's not that the skeptics care less about improving people's lives; surely it's fair to say that no one enters the field of foreign aid without a genuine desire to make a difference. Where the schism lies is in how the mission of aid is defined.

For some, providing aid is a means, not an end. It is a tool to be leveraged in order to advance other goals and interests. That such investments have the potential to help people is seen as a benefit, to be sure, but one that is tangential to the broader mission.

During the Bush administration, Michael and his colleagues found that an older mind-set—emphasizing inputs rather than outputs, and preferring traditional ways of doing business—required new proposals to come in the form of presidential initiatives, which often amounted to a kind of ad hoc aid reform. When the Obama administration brought Raj into USAID, resisting and transforming that mind-set became, in many ways, his central task. And when he left the agency, he did so with the confidence that his replacement would bring the same worldview and commitment to the task. One exceptional leader, Admiral Tim Ziemer, implemented the President's Malaria Initiative during both administrations, with tremendous competence and quiet passion.

Still, though a great deal of progress has been made, what happens next will depend largely on the kind of people appointed by subsequent administrations to lead these programs. In government, gravity is a very powerful force; the boulder won't make it up the hill unless someone is willing to push it. We, the authors, believe it is critical to choose people for these roles who fully embrace the need for a results-oriented aid strategy. But we are also deeply cognizant of the challenges these people will face. We know full well that having a worldview and implementing a worldview are two very different things.

First, and somewhat ironically, the people in charge of depoliticizing the aid process are going to need considerable political sophistication. As we can attest, both the American political environment and the complex political currents in partner countries often require a measure of diplomacy. In order to keep the constituency for aid as broad as possible, the people tasked with leading these initiatives need to be nimble enough to avoid unnecessary political pitfalls.

They also need to have a real fluency in the art and craft of aid. Development, after all, is a discipline. Over the course of fifty years, a lot of research and writing and results have issued from this nation's development experiences. Our leaders have gained insights from great successes and great failures, been surprised by the results of randomized controlled trials, and built a canon of wisdom that is now taught at the very best policy schools in the country. In such a complicated environment, expertise cannot be optional.

Lastly, we need leaders in those positions who have a personal, relentless, consuming passion for the task of saving and improving lives. Because at the end of the day, Congress and foreign aid coalitions respond to leadership that is grounded in conviction and purpose. This is the kind of work that offers the possibility of global transformation, of saving lives and changing futures on a massive scale. It is a mission larger than our everyday political disagreements, and it involves a moral calling shared across parties and ideologies.

4. WE MUST DESIGN STRATEGIES THAT FOCUS ON MEASURABLE OUTCOMES.

With leaders in place as described above, the next task is to incorporate a demand for results at the very heart of aid policy, weaving measurement and accountability into the fabric of aid programs. As our fellow authors noted in earlier chapters, this is the key to Moneyball—making sure that as development leaders, we can confidently say that it was our program, and not some other factor, that caused the effect we measure.

In foreign assistance, one of the most powerful ways to ascertain that assurance is through quasi-experimentation: a process that compares the outcomes for people who received an intervention with the outcomes for those similarly situated who did not. One of the most powerful examples of this concerned the horrific famine that visited Ethiopia between 1983 and 1985. In those years, Ethiopia had very little foreign assistance to speak of. It lacked the infrastructure and the agricultural capacity to withstand a severe change in weather. And it lacked the health services to prevent starvation and disease. The result was devastating. Hundreds of thousands of men, women, and children died slowly and painfully while the rest of the world watched in horror.

In the decade that followed, America, the UK, and the World Bank invested substantial funds in half a dozen major initiatives in Ethiopia, with the goal of preventing the next famine. Together, we put programs in place that improved agricultural productivity by a massive factor. We transformed the Ethiopian health system so that children in the country were immunized, because we knew that diseases, not starvation, are what ultimately kill most children during a famine. We developed inexpensive field tools to determine the degree of a child's malnourishment, measuring the circumference of arms and heads rather than taking blood and sending it to a lab.

When President Obama took office in 2009, he built on these efforts, introducing a program called Feed the Future that, like PEPFAR, was designed to be results oriented. The administration invested in baseline surveys in each country in order to measure the program's impact. The administration selected several countries, including Ethiopia, based on their willingness to change policies, fight corruption, and increase their own domestic investment in agriculture.

Then in 2011, these efforts were put to the test.

A quarter century after the 1984 famine, the same kind of weather patterns emerged in the region. Months of dry weather created the worst drought in nearly sixty years. Crops and livestock were decimated. As food stores came under strain, the price of food around the Horn of Africa began skyrocketing, forcing many to flee. A stream of refugees began pouring into overcrowded camps, leading to outbreaks of measles and cholera. More than 12 million people were at risk and in need of aid—many of them malnourished children.[73]

But unlike in 1984, in 2011 there was no famine in Ethiopia. No humanitarian crisis. On the contrary: over the next three years, instead of seeing a sharp increase in chronic malnutrition, Ethiopia experienced a 9 percent reduction.[74]

These results are immensely powerful. They not only confirm that foreign assistance efforts in Ethiopia worked, but they also give us a model for fighting hunger in other parts of the world.

If foreign aid agencies continue funding results-oriented programs, we'll have more and more opportunities to measure the relative effectiveness of our strategies. Over time, we'll be able to create a development playbook, ensuring that we are using the very best tools to implement the most effective programs everywhere that we take action.

5. WE MUST RESIST THE PRESSURE TO REVERT TO OLD PRACTICES THAT DON'T RELY ON DATA AND EVIDENCE TO ACHIEVE RESULTS.

When Raj was at USAID, rarely a day went by when he didn't find himself under enormous pressure to backslide into the very practices he was fighting against. Sometimes that pressure would come from within government—for example, the Department of Defense would ask USAID to build a project for another country's military as an exercise in alliance building. But these expenses, even if justifiable from a military perspective, ran counter to the development assistance mission. In such circumstances, resisting pressure is as difficult as it is essential.

It is the responsibility of the president's national security team to understand, appreciate, and protect the role of foreign assistance as a results-oriented tool. But in both Michael's and Raj's experience, there is a temptation among national security professionals to view foreign assistance as a consolation prize: "We can't send our military in. What else can we do?"

Pressure can be relentless also from representatives of foreign governments. Raj recalls a series of disagreements with the Pakistani foreign minister, for instance, over how and where aid should be spent in the country. The foreign minister was adamant that the U.S. not spend aid money on health and education despite the country having some of the very worst outcomes in both categories. "Health and education are provincial responsibilities," she would explain. "So you're not actually helping the government of Pakistan by sending money there."

Other times, the Pakistani government would push back on both what USAID was funding and where. Officials would request that the organization stop spending money on programs in the provinces of the president's political opponents. They had alternative suggestions on how we might better invest our aid—on an infrastructure project in Islamabad, perhaps, or on an energy project that would benefit a particularly favored company.

Simply put, the purpose of foreign assistance should be to save and improve the lives of the people, and development leaders cannot allow competing political priorities to compromise that mission. Again, this may seem obvious, but it remains a countercultural point of view within the aid and foreign policy communities.

If you talk to experts in this field, and if you read the literature and listen to the public remarks, much of what you'll hear is about making sure that the ambition of American aid is aligned with the interests of the country in which we are working. On its face, this makes a great deal of sense. But in reality, there are a lot of cases, particularly in those places most desperate for aid, where a political leader's priority is to stay in power rather than to help his or her people. Foreign assistance cannot become a blank check used to purchase friends or pay off enemies. Assistance programs should be designed in partnership with countries, but both sides must prioritize delivering results that improve the health and welfare of the population—particularly the poor.

It's also important that the United States does not threaten to cut spending on essential aid programs, even in countries where tensions may arise. We need to avoid using health and development assistance as a stick for our enemies, in the same way we must avoid using it purely as a carrot.

Egypt may be the perfect illustration. A lot of USAID engagements in Egypt are very results oriented and have proven to be very effective. One study of the twenty-five-year impact of USAID in Egypt shows staggering improvements in girls' education levels, women's labor force participation levels, and public sanitation in urban settings.[75] In fact, because of this work, health and basic health access indicators for women and girls aren't just high in the context of Egypt; controlling for income, they are higher than in any other part of the Middle East.

This goal would never have been achieved if USAID had failed to maintain a consistent, long-term focus on results. It is one thing, in the aftermath of a coup, to threaten the end of military assistance (withholding fighter jets, for example). But we should not—and we did not—make the same threat with a national-level girls' education program.

6. WE MUST PROTECT SPENDING ON RESULTS-ORIENTED AID AND ASSISTANCE.

Whether spending is on agriculture or education, on water or sanitation, we know which characteristics deliver results: country ownership and leadership, a commitment on the ground to measurements and reporting, and a willingness to identify what doesn't work and to make changes. Much of this critical work can be done only by and with America's country partners, which are showing tremendous innovation and leadership in many policy areas. We see Bangladesh working on its own evidence-informed climate resilience campaign, while El Salvador works on crime prevention and public safety. We see Brazil successfully ending large-scale hunger through investment in hunger and nutrition programs, while Colombia concentrates on rural development as part of achieving peace and reconciliation. Our job as development leaders is to protect and support the people on the ground who are brave and willing and focused on results, because effective aid is a full partnership.

At the same time, we must acknowledge that no such partnership can work if it isn't funded. The two of us, of course, come from different political parties and probably would disagree on many issues concerning federal spending. But we are completely aligned in the belief that results-oriented programs should not go unfunded or underfunded. Not when we know they work. Not when they are saving millions of lives every year. Not when spending on all foreign assistance amounts to less than 1 percent of the federal budget. The idea is risible that America has a budget problem because it gives out too many insecticide-treated bed nets or provides too much AIDS treatment.

We also appreciate that in times of budget constraint, increases in foreign assistance may be hard to come by. It will be necessary to make every dollar count. The key, ultimately, is to ensure that programs offering proven, measurable outcomes are given the space and resources to continue. And by the same token, the U.S. ought to be sure that money spent on ineffective programs is reallocated so that the impact we want is the impact we actually achieve.

7. WE MUST DEVELOP EFFECTIVE CONFLICT-ZONE STRATEGIES USING THE BEST DATA AND EVIDENCE AVAILABLE.

Much of the mantra of effectiveness and results grew out of work done in the mid-1990s, which showed that where you have stable governments, better policy environments, and more natural and human resources, aid dollars go further. This means you are likely to get better health outcomes for your health investments in Tanzania, for example, than in Somalia.

This rather obvious point became a rigorous focus of development economics for more than a decade, and it helped determine how capital allocations are made in the field. The World Bank, for example, adopted a country performance index assessment and started shifting money to those countries with better policy environments. The Millennium Challenge Corporation (MCC) did something similar for American economic aid. In that program, a board certifies countries that are likely to use aid wisely—nations committed to democratic and free market reform and to fighting corruption—and works with them as partners on projects to combat poverty and encourage economic growth. Nations that backtrack on reform and good governance have their "compacts" cut off.

This effort, by and large, has produced excellent results. The global competition for MCC compacts has been vigorous, with nations willing to make serious reforms—on corruption, land rights, women's rights, and other rule-of-law issues—in order to receive them. After Malawi failed to meet the eligibility criteria on corruption in 2004, for example, the government passed legislation to combat money laundering, prevent financing of terrorism, and require the declaration of assets by public officials. Malawi also implemented a new financial management and reporting system to increase transparency and accountability.

But there are limits to a policy of reward for good government, set principally by the emerging reality of global poverty. It is true that nearly a billion people have risen out of poverty over the past two decades, with the most remarkable gains coming in China and India. The next round of progress against poverty is likely to come harder, however. When you look at some of the foreign aid community's more ambitious goals—such as ending extreme poverty by 2030—you quickly realize that the bulk of the billions of people who survive on $1.25 or less a day are living either in conflict zones or in fragile countries. Some live in countries with very corrupt governance systems; others, in places with no system of governance at all. Fragile states are where the future of poverty lies.

And so the key insight from recent development efforts—this notion that aid is more effective if provided in better places—is no longer particularly valuable to our broader aims. To be successful at reaching the sustainable development goals the world has set forth, foreign assistance organizations are going to need to figure out how to drive success in places where that success will always be harder-won. Working in fragile states is expensive compared with development efforts in stable countries. Security concerns often limit the involvement of nongovernmental partners. And development interventions, often focused on building resilience, demand specialized skills.

This may very well be the greatest development challenge the foreign aid community faces. But working in fragile states represents a commitment to fight poverty where it is found—and success in these areas is not irrelevant to important national purposes. Weak and failed states often collect problems, from pandemic disease to sexual violence to ideological radicalization. The next generation of those who fight extreme poverty will need the skills and courage to work in the world's broken places.

They will also need a strategy.

The foreign assistance community has learned a lot in recent decades—both from success and from failure—about what it takes to do development work in conflict zones. We know, first and foremost, that development can deliver results even in the most hostile environments. Our efforts to improve health care outcomes in Afghanistan, for example, have expanded access to basic primary care from almost none of the population after the fall of the Taliban to more than 80 percent of the population.[76] And that has been correlated with the largest, deepest, and fastest reductions in child mortality and maternal mortality anywhere in the world over the past decade.

This isn't just a development strategy; it's a governance strategy. Indeed, for all the work we've done in Afghanistan trying to build governing capacity—from helping its leaders create a government to training civil workers to manage that government—it is likely that more has been done to build Afghanistan's governance capacity by getting 8 million kids in school, including more than 2.5 million girls.[77] Building a just and stable political order in a conflict zone may take decades, but it starts, fundamentally, by making sure a country's children are taught and fed and vaccinated. The goal in a conflict zone, we've learned, should be to focus on things that are measurable and meaningful, such as education and health and energy access. And there is a fair amount of evidence to suggest that development begets development—that interventions to manage one kind of crisis can prepare even the most fragile countries to defend against another.

In 2014, when the Ebola pandemic ravaged the post-conflict nations of Liberia, Sierra Leone, and Guinea, the extraordinary fragility of these countries and their health systems—despite developmental efforts and investments in health care—exposed the entire world to a pandemic threat. After a massive international effort, Ebola was contained and, ultimately, nearly resolved in West Africa, but not until nearly 30,000 people were infected and 11,000 victims lost their lives.[78]

What the three affected nations had in common was a health care system with minimal capacity. Each country had very few doctors and health care workers, many of whom died trying to care for the sick and deceased. As a result, a localized epidemic became a global pandemic risk. Meanwhile, nearby countries that had a higher level of capacity and appropriate international support were able to successfully prevent the spread of this terrible disease.

There were nearly 4,000 cases of Ebola in Guinea, but only one case in neighboring Senegal.[79] Sierra Leone had more than 13,000 cases, while Mali had just 8.[80] And Nigeria, the continent's most populous country, reported just 20 cases.[81] What allowed countries like Mali, with an annual per capita income of $775, and Nigeria, where Boko Haram continues to create tremendous instability in the north, to marshal a response so much more effectively than Sierra Leone, a country that is equally poor? The difference, it appears, lies in the health and development partnerships already established there. Nigeria, Mali, and Senegal had PEPFAR programs in place. Each was part of the President's Malaria Initiative. Each had seen large health system investments aimed at improving child survival rates. The efforts of the Global Polio Eradication Initiative in Nigeria proved particularly critical, bringing basic capabilities: an emergency operations center, a focused effort to reach at-risk households, and a well-funded international program with trained local staff.

In contrast, efforts to build health systems in Guinea, Sierra Leone, and Liberia were less focused, less well resourced, and less effective. The international effort to beat back Ebola in these nations ultimately required thousands of personnel and billions of dollars, and it came at immense cost to the international community. It is now imperative that we learn from these experiences. The thousands of trained health care personnel who have helped fight Ebola can be transformed into a network of community health workers who serve as the basis of a new public health infrastructure in these nations. The labs, operations centers, and logistics systems put in place for just such an emergency could refocus on saving children from everyday killers: malaria, diarrhea, pneumonia, and (along with their mothers) childbirth.

This is not a conflict-zone assistance strategy. At this stage, the only thing we can say with confidence is that there is no clear set of solutions that has worked consistently in the past. Events in Yemen, Somalia, Libya, and northern Nigeria all serve as proof that we must create a new set of tools, strategies, and capabilities to achieve development goals in difficult environments. A critical task for the next administration is to continue innovating and experimenting in this area—to build the data, analyze the evidence, and help devise strategies and capabilities that can work reliably—even in the world's harshest places.

A NEW ERA OF AID

Because this field is so dominated by well-meaning technical people, they sometimes forget that there is an essential political task to be accomplished. Very often in the past, we have lacked a political consensus on the value of aid—not just what it is worth, but whether it's worth anything at all. That skepticism is sometimes rooted in ideology, but more often than not it is a response to the perception of past failure. If the goal of foreign aid is merely to improve America's approval ratings around the world, then it's easy to dismiss our efforts thus far as either ineffective or optional.

What is required, then, is not just a transformation in the way we approach foreign assistance, but a different way of thinking and talking from leaders on both sides of the aisle. We need Democrats to acknowledge that bad aid policy has failed in the past, and we need Republicans to acknowledge the power and importance of smartly run, data-driven aid programs.

But even more important, we need to see beyond our traditional party politics, to understand that on these issues, our common ground is vast. This is an issue where evangelicals and atheists can hold hands in common cause. Smart aid is smart politics whether you're a Democrat or a Republican. It's smart policy whether you're a liberal or a conservative. It's smart diplomacy whether you're a hawk or a dove. There is so much work still to be done. If, as President Kennedy urged, we are going to be wise leaders and good neighbors, it's best we do it together.

Chapter VII.

A CALL TO PLAY BALL

By U.S. Senator **Kelly Ayotte** (R-NH)

U.S. Senator **Mark Warner** (D-VA)

We started this book with a description of an impressive winning streak—the longest in the history of the American League. A made-for-Hollywood, feel-good, David-and-Goliath tale. But before Billy Beane's A's were winning, they were losing. Big time.

At the beginning of the 2002 Moneyball season, the A's went 5-16. They were swept by the middling Toronto Blue Jays. Swept by Kelly's Boston Red Sox—*at home*. They lost seven consecutive series for the first time in eight years, and the criticism and finger-pointing was endless.

"There may not be an *A* in *quit*, as the team advertising campaign claims. But there is an *A* in *awful*," one sportswriter observed. "There's no *A* in *quit*, but there is an *A* in *hapless*," another piled on a few days later.

"Ask anybody associated with the A's what's wrong with the team these days . . . and check out the puzzled expression you get. Maybe a better question is, 'What's not wrong?'" commented a third.

At that time, Beane's revolutionary data-driven, evidence-based methodology was considered a half-baked fantasy—a punch line.

We know the feeling—because we hear those criticisms every day about the performance of our federal government. We hear that this Congress is the least productive in history, that nothing will ever get done. Over the past few years of partisanship and gridlock, congressional approval has dropped below that of the big banks and used-car salesmen. According to a Gallup poll, Congress is less popular than colonoscopies and root canals.[82] As our colleague Senator John McCain (R-AZ) is fond of saying, we're down to just blood relatives.

Certainly, the anger and frustration is understandable. Given all the dysfunction, it's easy to assume that nothing productive will ever come out of a Washington this broken. But while it would be easy to assume that, it would also be wrong.

In fact, we've witnessed some important moments in recent years proving that there are still ideas—sometimes very big ideas—that can win bipartisan support. In 2012, legislators on both sides of the aisle came together to reform securities regulations and make it easier for fledgling start-up businesses to succeed; we called it the JOBS Act. During the summer of 2014, Congress again came together to overhaul and update our job-training programs for the twenty-first century; the vote was 415-6 in the House, 95-3 in the Senate.

This chapter isn't even the only thing the two of us have coauthored. As the leaders of the Senate Budget Committee's Government Performance Task Force, we are cosponsors of a bill that would eliminate or consolidate more than three hundred reports—produced by more than two dozen federal agencies—that have been found to be unnecessary, duplicative, or outdated. In addition, we passed the groundbreaking Digital Accountability and Transparency Act. Our bipartisan legislation standardizes federal spending data and ensures that it is available online so taxpayers can access information about how their tax dollars are being spent, and we can use this data to better inform decision making across government.

Of course, we don't always see eye to eye on every issue, but we've come to appreciate and respect one another's views. We actually enjoy figuring out how we can work together to move America forward. And while we'd like to think we're especially committed to working productively across the aisle, we also know that we're not alone in doing so. To paraphrase Mark Twain, rumors of the death of bipartisanship have been greatly exaggerated.

What the authors of this book have done so well is to show three things. First, they've demonstrated that we can—and should— use evidence and data about what works to improve the lives of young people and their families. With so much at stake—measured not just in dollars but also in the well-being of Americans—it's not enough to keep groping in the dark for solutions. We have to demand more. We need to kick the status quo to the curb and elevate evidence in our country to create real change. That means revamping our approach toward policy making and budget decisions, ensuring that the right information gets into the right decision makers' hands at the right time. This is not about passing one bill or signing a few executive orders; it's about transforming the process by which we make decisions.

Second, we don't all need to agree on everything politically in order to agree to use evidence more effectively. Moneyball doesn't require Washington to reach a consensus on health-care reform or defense spending. But it does require that we introduce more objective evidence and data into our policy-making process and budget decisions, even as we continue to debate what those policies and dollar allocations should be. Our choices should be more informed by what will have the most impact and have the best results.

Third, this book illustrates—provides evidence, you could say—that Moneyball is in the best interest of both Democrats and Republicans, and, more importantly, of the nation as a whole. It gives Republicans a chance to strip out unnecessary programs and prove that smaller government is effective government. It gives Democrats the opportunity to prove that government, irrespective of its size, can help improve outcomes for Americans of all walks of life. And does anyone doubt that such a commitment from both parties would yield a smarter, more useful, more compassionate government? What Thomas Jefferson called, more than two centuries ago, "a wise and frugal government"?

In short, neither of us is naïve about the historic challenges facing the legislative body in which we are privileged to serve, nor about the polarization that has pervaded it in recent years. And yet we are still deeply optimistic about Moneyball's prospects.

There's a big difference, however, between being confident that we *can* get this done and being confident that we *will* get it done. Of roughly ten thousand bills introduced every session, only about 5 percent will ever become law.

If we have any hope of bridging the gap between ideas and implementation—of overcoming the inertia and bias toward inaction—then we need people to take action. This cannot be the project of a passionate few. It must be a cause taken up and championed by millions of Americans, Left and Right, in Congress and across the country.

So to our fellow members of Congress, we ask you to join us as we raise awareness about the need to use evidence and data to make better, more-informed decisions. On your committees and in your own legislation, push for the programs you authorize and fund to be rigorously evaluated—for the sake of the taxpayers and everyone who might benefit from these programs. Help us figure out if what we're doing is working.

To the president, presidential candidates, and every agency of the federal government, build on the work you're already doing. In dozens of small but significant ways, the Bush and Obama administrations embraced Moneyball—so now let's scale it. Turn evidence-based pilot programs into major initiatives. Make these efforts the centerpiece of a more effective administration, from the Department of Defense to the Department of Health and Human Services. Find room in your budgets for evidence, because doing so will create *more* room in the budget. Don't be content just to mindlessly slash or grow the federal government—streamline it. Test it. Fine-tune it. *Fix* it.

To the pundits and opinion makers on our TVs and op-ed pages, give Moneyball a chance. Go beyond the talking points and shouting matches that pass for discourse these days and seriously engage with the issue. Examine our proposal. Question it. Help explain it fairly and objectively to the American people. But reserve your skepticism and don't summarily dismiss it as a pipe dream.

Just remember: the scouts and sportswriters initially doubted Billy Beane's methods, too.

To the cities, states, foundations, and nonprofits whose work we have highlighted, keep moving forward. Continue incubating and innovating these extraordinary programs. Test your health-care programs and preschools; gather and analyze data on unemployment and homelessness and recidivism. Demonstrate every day that data and evidence can—and does—change outcomes and lift the lives of people all across America. Brick by evidentiary brick, help us build support for Moneyball at the highest levels of government. Because when we marshal data to persuade people of the effectiveness of evidence-based policy making, it is to your progress that we point.

Lastly, to you, the reader—and every citizen of this great nation—continue caring about honest, effective government. Demand accountability, demand investment in what works, and demand that we break free from the tired debate that has dragged us through some of the worst partisan warfare in recent memory. You care about where your tax dollars are going, and you have a right to, so don't let Washington hijack that conversation for cynical, partisan ends. For starters, visit MoneyballForGov.com and sign on to our Moneyball principles. Join this movement and help us move it forward—so that together we can move the country forward.

After too many years of hand-wringing and wishful thinking, it's time to reimagine how government can work on behalf of children and families and communities. It's time to move from an approach that serves only to further polarize our political process to one that works productively to better the lives of all Americans. A decade and a half into the twenty-first century, the batter's up and the bases are loaded. It's time to play Moneyball.

Afterword

A BIPARTISAN MONEYBALL AGENDA [83]

By   **Robert Gordon**
Former executive associate director at the Office of
Management and Budget

Ron Haskins
Senior fellow at the Brookings Institution

*We asked two scholars, **Robert Gordon**, a Democrat who worked in the Obama White House, and **Ron Haskins**, a Republican who worked in the Bush White House, to put together a broad agenda of policy proposals for Moneyball. And we asked them to keep a key question in mind as they developed it: What are the most practical and the most bipartisan steps we can take at the federal level to make Moneyball our reality?*

O ver the last two decades, government has made real progress in playing Moneyball. Some programs now tell potential grantees that they need to bring the evidence if they're going to get the money. A few agencies support research institutes that fund, analyze, and publicly present rigorous research. Social programs now use far more data to support their efforts than even a decade ago.

But use of evidence and data still isn't the norm for government. When we go into the drugstore and pick up some medicine, we know the company that manufactured it has conducted gold-standard research to demonstrate that the drug is safe and, at least in important cases, effective. When we log on to Amazon, we know that they are using enormous amounts of data to tailor their suggestions to our interests. (How we feel about that is a different issue.) But when we interact with a typical government program, we don't expect—and don't receive—the same effective and refined use of research.

History shows that government can raise its game. It used to be that a new mayor or governor or president could hire or fire staff at will based on party loyalty. The creation of the civil service, whatever its flaws, ended that practice. It used to be that government officials who expensed personal items would usually get away with it. Improvements in accounting, together with independent watchdogs like inspectors general, have curtailed those abuses. Pharmaceutical companies always test drugs because the law requires it.

New laws and organizations can help increase the use of evidence, but they won't be enough. There must be changes in leadership and culture. In this afterword, we outline some ideas for this transformation. They fall into three categories:

- Building leadership and infrastructure
- Transforming federal programs to learn and fund what works
- Moving funds from less-effective to more-effective programs

These three nuts-and-bolts proposals cover a lot of ground, but they are united by four pillars that should guide all decisions at every level of government. Here they are:

Pillar 1: Relentlessly use data and evaluation to learn from experience. Without a way of identifying what works and what doesn't, progress in social policy is impossible. Until recently, the most sophisticated evaluations required a lot of time and money. Sometimes that's still true, but not always. With modern data systems, we can do quick, sophisticated tests of different program designs. Think about a store chain testing different product placements in different stores—or a social-services agency testing different intake routines in different offices. To figure out cheaply what works, we can often use data that governments already collect. Think about a new math textbook: rather than setting up a whole new approach to collecting data, we can just assign the book to half the classes (selected at random) in a district and compare the scores of kids who used the new text with the scores of those who didn't, on tests the kids already take. And once we learn the best interventions, we can subject them to financial analysis to compare benefits and costs—and thus give policy makers an important tool to help make tough choices about different ways to spend limited resources.

Pillar 2: Define success in terms of measurable, transparent outcomes. Programs need goals for improving the world—not just spending money, providing services, or following rules. To summon public pressure for results, there should be clarity and openness about what these goals are and whether programs are achieving them.

Pillar 3: Create incentives to do what works. In a well-functioning market, companies that satisfy their customers and turn a profit grow, while less successful firms either improve or die. Sometimes public-sector programs can successfully simulate this environment by conditioning public funding on outcomes. This is often the right way to go. Yet there can also be practical challenges. Success may only become clear over a long period (think of preschool programs that aim, among other things, to increase college enrollment and completion), while funding decisions have to be made now. If too much depends on outcome metrics that lack great sophistication, gaming the system becomes a problem. For these reasons, rather than tying too much to measurable outcomes, it often makes sense to incentivize evidence-based program designs that are likely to achieve those outcomes.

Pillar 4: Foster innovation by cutting mandates and using waivers. Good people trying to get good results in diverse circumstances will often figure out better solutions than Washington can. The federal government needs to overcome its habit of viewing long rulebooks as paths to program improvement. Once there are good outcome incentives in place, hard-and-fast rules should be linked to essentials for protecting health and safety, avoiding the misappropriation of funds, or guaranteeing a national floor of benefits or services. Sometimes eliminating requirements for everyone and putting faith in local flexibility and measurement of outcomes will make sense. Other times, where accountability is weaker, it may be wiser to waive program rules for selected states or grantees that agree to adopt stronger metrics in a particular context.

RECOMMENDATIONS

Now to our recommendations. Just a note about scope: We focus on social interventions that are central to expanding individual opportunity. But we believe that these recommendations have application to most domestic policies—certainly to efforts aimed at creating jobs, for example—and to some foreign policies as well, notably foreign aid.

BUILDING LEADERSHIP AND INFRASTRUCTURE

Recommendation 1: Create a chief evaluation officer of the United States—and for every agency. Just as the Oakland Athletics wouldn't have succeeded at Moneyball without Billy Beane, government's efforts won't succeed without strong senior managers who have the power to make and back up decisions. There are too many pressures on decision makers that go beyond focusing on outcomes. So the executive branch needs a leader and small staff to captain Moneyball initiatives, and then each agency needs the same kind of team.

This does not require a bigger bureaucracy. The Office of Management and Budget (OMB) already works to drive evaluation work, but the office has an immense range of mandates, and the Moneyball agenda rises and falls with different directors. Talented career staff contribute a lot, but many of them have other "real jobs." To institutionalize Moneyball, OMB needs a chief evaluation officer who can provide expert advice to the OMB director and senior agency leadership on how to integrate research into decision making and who can coordinate data, evaluation, and performance management to strengthen agency capacity for learning. This would combine, in one elevated role, two separate jobs in recent years: the executive associate director and the associate director for performance management.

Like OMB, most agencies today have evaluation units, but some lack sufficiently senior leadership. In others, out of an admirable desire to ensure that research isn't politicized, key evaluators play only a modest role in designing programs—including their evaluations. But policy makers and program designers need input from evaluators to do their jobs well. And each agency needs a chief evaluation officer reporting to the secretary or deputy secretary.

Agencies can make changes to get this done. In recent years, the Department of Labor did not have a strong culture of evaluation. But in President Obama's first term, the department's leadership hired distinguished chief evaluation officers, first Jean Grossman from Princeton and then Demetra Nightingale from the Urban Institute. Deputy Secretary Seth Harris required every bureau to work with the chief evaluation officers and develop a learning agenda to identify what works in priority areas. Today evidence and evaluation are parts of every discretionary grant program at the department. Moreover, the department initiated two major evidence-based programs and one of the first federal Pay for Success initiatives. If other federal agencies had similarly empowered leaders, they could produce similar results.

Recommendation 2: Set aside up to 1 percent for evaluation at each agency. According to a recent GAO report, only 37 percent of government program managers said that an evaluation of their programs had been completed in the last five years. That's disturbing but not surprising. Historically, evaluation has often been lumped with program administration that nobody likes to fund.

This attitude is understandable but misguided. The private sector spends well over 12 percent of all its domestic investment on R&D, and the amount of investment has been increasing since 1950. But at agencies like the Department of Education, R&D is well under 1 percent of discretionary spending.

To make sure every agency can access the funding it needs for evaluation, with the flexibility to spend it well, agencies should have authority to direct up to 1 percent of their total discretionary funds toward program evaluation. While many agencies would choose to spend less in some years, the authority would help ensure that the agency did not miss important learning opportunities when they arise. Agencies could draw the funds from across each discretionary program on an equal basis and then spend on the highest-priority evaluations, subject to congressional oversight. The Department of Labor now has an authority along these lines, and other agencies should get it, too.

Recommendation 3: Create cross-government prizes for innovative approaches to evaluation. Agencies also need incentives to commit more energy to evaluation. Early in the Obama administration, OMB ran a competition for the best evaluation ideas, then put winning proposals into its budget. The competition stimulated excellent new thinking but lost momentum after Congress failed to appropriate funding. More recently, the Coalition for Evidence-Based Policy has demonstrated the power of a fully funded prize to elicit new ideas for evaluations: $300,000 in prize money this year drew fifty-three prize proposals for low-cost randomized controlled trials (RCTs) in important policy areas. While the coalition has adequate funding to award only three prizes, some of the runners-up are likely to be funded by philanthropy or government.

Building on these examples, Congress should appropriate a small amount of funds for OMB to allocate for critical advances in evaluation. In some instances, OMB could help agencies strengthen their capacity for low-cost randomized controlled trials and rapid-cycle evaluations, especially if administrative data can be used as outcome measures. In other cases, OMB could guarantee funding for evaluations that answer critical questions that drive policy decisions. An OMB-run allocation process would provide added support for evaluators within agencies, ensure that cutting-edge initiatives receive funding, and provide a forum for shared learning across and beyond government. Indeed, the review of applications could be a public conversation with experts outside government that eventually attracts philanthropic and university support.

Recommendation 4: Create comprehensive, easy-to-use "what works" databases at each agency—and develop a gateway for searching them all. It's not enough to evaluate programs if nobody knows about the results. The evidence about what works needs to be available in a single place, online, in a format that is true to the research but accessible to laypeople, especially policy makers and their staffs. Every government-funded study needs to be accounted for, including studies that are ongoing, so there is no question whether results are being suppressed. And such an Internet source should set high standards before suggesting conclusions.

Putting evaluations online, with high evidence standards, can inform better decision making and signal to researchers the importance of using rigorous research and evaluation designs. Before the What Works Clearinghouse (WWC) of the Institute of Education Sciences (IES), there was a powerful tendency in education to blur the distinction among types of research. An RCT using validated performance measures might be viewed as no more meaningful than an after-the-fact survey of program participants. These would be "two conflicting studies." The WWC lifted standards and clarified which programs were supported by rigorous research evidence and which were not. There is still real work to do—particularly in emphasizing the importance of effects. But the WWC is real progress.

In the last few years, other agencies and programs have followed suit, creating similarly comprehensive online resources in areas as diverse as home visiting and job training. But there are still no "what works" databases for huge swaths of federal programs, including much of health, housing, and national-service initiatives. Even among agencies that have established clearinghouses, none identifies all government-funded, ongoing, or completed research online in one place. And the databases are separate, even though researchers and practitioners often work across issue areas.

Most important, information is not always accessible to practitioners and actionable on the ground. There need to be more step-by-step guides showing people how to apply successes from elsewhere in their circumstances, or, even more effective, access to coaching, webinars, or other tools to help community and nonprofit leaders understand successful implementation. This will require a new level of collaboration among policy makers, program managers, and evaluators. Government should set aside a little funding, then partner with philanthropy to facilitate the development of cross-subject platforms, user-friendly websites, and high-quality support for implementation. The Pew-MacArthur Results First Initiative is a great first step here and should serve as a model for other foundations.

Recommendation 5: Create and institutionalize "Moneyball scores"—showing not just what works, but what works best for the money. Using evidence is a solid step forward, but policy makers and practitioners also need to know if the program they are evaluating works better for the money than the alternatives. This is called cost-benefit analysis or "return on investment" analysis.

How do we quantify the benefits from improving a child's reading, or stopping a violent crime, or saving a life? These are fraught questions. But we're answering many of them today in other contexts. Since the Reagan administration, a part of the Office of Management and Budget called the Office of Information and Regulatory Affairs (OIRA) has estimated the social costs and benefits from different regulations. While policies can advance human dignity in important ways that cost-benefit analysis doesn't capture, OIRA is often able to apply a simple principle: a regulation shouldn't go forward unless the benefits exceed the costs. Over the last ten years, officials in both Democratic and Republican administrations have reported that regulatory efforts have produced hundreds of billions of dollars in net benefits.[84]

While there are many challenges, a similar process could apply to federal grants. The Robin Hood Foundation, which fights poverty in New York City, already uses cost-benefit analysis to compare interventions across diverse domains. And the Washington State Institute for Public Policy has developed cost-benefit estimates for a range of interventions, from reducing criminal recidivism to expanding access to early-childhood education. The Washington State legislature—and now, legislatures in about a dozen other states, thanks to the Pew-MacArthur Results First Initiative—is using cost-benefit analysis to consider whether its own social investments are getting results.[85]

Because of the complexity and controversy inherent in cost-benefit analysis, the federal government will need a nonpolitical expert entity to design principles with substantial public input. The Institute of Medicine, with funding from the MacArthur Foundation, is now convening an expert panel to develop common principles for analyzing prevention programs. While there will never be universal agreement on methodology, either that body or another should continue and broaden its work until there is a widely endorsed approach to producing estimates (or ranges of estimates) of costs and benefits for a broad array of social-intervention programs.

At that point, both executive and congressional analysts should begin to employ cost-benefit approaches in providing Moneyball scores for legislation. Nobody does that today. The Congressional Budget Office focuses on the costs of legislation but only sometimes looks at benefits. For example, CBO will show savings to the government in a program that is permanently funded but not one that is funded each year. CBO's mandate should be broadened—or a new office created—to report on the evidence supporting different initiatives and to consider the broad costs and benefits from government expenditures.

Executive agencies should also create Moneyball scores to evaluate different grantees. In addition to determining whether a program is using an approach that gets results, an agency would determine how the cost per outcome in that program stacks up against other programs serving similar populations.

Recommendation 6: Build crosscutting data systems that also protect privacy. The key to Moneyball for government is data—especially low-cost data. In recent years, governments at all levels have been increasing their investments in building systems to collect data, protect it, and match it across domains (education, labor, health, etc.). The Obama administration has created a default policy of making government data sets available to the public. Many cities are building their own open data platforms.

But there is still a great deal of work to do. Too often, key data systems are not connected. For example, evaluations of postsecondary-education training programs would ideally reflect baseline information about high school achievement, as well as subsequent employment outcomes. Evaluations of elementary-school interventions would similarly draw on background data from social-services systems. Yet this is often impossible because of policies restricting data sharing.

One problem here is cost. Early in the Obama administration, Congress invested strongly in strengthening longitudinal data systems in both education and worker training. But as discretionary spending has come under tight caps, this funding has largely dried up.

While it makes sense to press harder for data-infrastructure funding, such an effort will run into real concerns about data privacy. Such fears sank inBloom, an effort to create an easy way for teachers to see the critical information about their students. The lesson here is that policy makers cannot expect to build data systems, show they work, and hope everyone will thank them. Instead, they need to address data issues up front, as systems are being built, in a way that conveys that the gains in efficiency from using data won't crowd out people's concerns about their dignity and privacy.

Representative Paul Ryan (R-WI) has a proposal for a Commission on Evidence-Based Policy Making with the charge to decide whether and how to bring together through a single clearinghouse multiple data sources—and to settle on the privacy protections for that database. Putting privacy issues at the center of the conversation can help ensure that the smart use of data gains broad support.

Recommendation 7: Build human capital in government. While Moneyball uses big data and advanced statistics, the endeavor ultimately depends on people. To take one example: rapid-cycle evaluation at a service-delivery agency requires policy experts to identify plausible new approaches; program managers to implement them; technologists to create or modernize data systems to capture effects; social scientists or statisticians to analyze the data on effects; and crosscutting leaders who know how to bring these pieces together with inspiration and precision.

Within government, increasing use of short-term fellowships and assignments from academic institutions can help build temporary expertise. But government needs outstanding individuals who dedicate many years to the work.

Unfortunately, governments at all levels increasingly struggle to get and keep the people they need. In part due to repeated pay freezes and shutdown crises, federal-employee job satisfaction is at its lowest level since 2003.[86] Attrition has risen 37 percent since 2009. While public-sector jobs always pay less than their private-sector counterparts, the gap is widening.[87] For employees with advanced degrees, average pay is now 18 percent below the private sector.[88] Attracting and retaining excellent staff is made more difficult by rules governing hiring, retention, and promotion that were developed for an industrial economy seventy years ago.

The Partnership for Public Service and others have proposed comprehensive reforms in the civil service, including changes in pay, hiring, and retention practices. These recommendations—and comparable efforts at the state and local levels—deserve a close look.[89]

TRANSFORMING FEDERAL PROGRAMS TO LEARN AND FUND WHAT WORKS

Recommendation 8: Protect, improve, and grow tiered-evidence programs. Building on a Bush administration concept, the Obama administration created six tiered-evidence programs across the federal government.[90] These programs represent a breakthrough because of two design features: First, they provide more money to programs with higher levels of evidence (hence the "tiers"), creating a strong incentive to do what works. Second, they require evaluations so that programs can continue learning and improving.

Even though these types of initiatives represent some of the best in government, their survival is far from assured. Neither of the evidence initiatives at the Department of Labor still exists in its original form. The key spending committee in the House of Representatives has previously targeted all of the programs for elimination. And because these programs are all creations of the Obama administration, they run the risk of being forgotten by the next president in either party regardless of their merits.

If we want a government that works, stepping back from tiered-evidence initiatives would be a terrible mistake. A recent review of the evidence-based education initiative noted that three of its four largest grantees have established strong positive outcomes in rigorous evaluations (and the fourth evaluation has not yet been completed). Across the six original initiatives, there are now around seven hundred programs being carried out, most with evaluations and many with RCTs. These will soon produce a whole new generation of evidence about what works. Other evidence-based initiatives for parental home visiting, teen-pregnancy prevention, and the Social Innovation Fund (SIF) have funded programs that have promising records of success.

As a more general matter, there's good reason to believe that at current funding levels, the evidence-based programs have a higher return on investment (ROI) than typical government programs. For example, based on nonexperimental research, the average federal job-training program has a modest positive ROI.[91] But job-training programs vary widely. Some are terrific, some are terrible, and most are in the middle. By prioritizing approaches proven to work, evidence-based workforce programs are likely to achieve higher average levels of impact. And the requirement to evaluate results will provide a basis to improve programs all along the spectrum of effectiveness.

To be sure, evidence-based initiatives still have room to improve. One recurring error is treating interventions as proven when their effects are *statistically* significant, even when some of those effects aren't so important for taxpayers. For example, take three home-visiting programs: One of the programs reduces infant mortality, a second reduces child abuse, and a third increases the number of referrals made to other providers. The first two programs get much more important results than the third, but currently the law treats all three programs as equally strong. That should change.

Even with improvements, the evidence initiatives have room to grow. In 2013, the Investing in Innovation Fund at the Department of Education had 618 applicants and made twenty-five grants, giving it an acceptance rate comparable to a highly selective college.[92] Many unfunded applicants received scores that were trivially different from winners. Similarly, evidence-based home-visitation programs currently serve a small fraction of low-income mothers who are eligible. Right now, it makes sense not only to protect these evidence-based initiatives but also to expand them.

Recommendation 9: Grow Pay for Success and scale what works for social mobility. While tiered-evidence initiatives require past records of success, they provide taxpayer money even if programs fail. A different approach, Pay for Success, goes a step further. Rather than pay for a service up front, the government enters an agreement to pay only after a program delivers specified results, usually results that save taxpayers money. Providers raise money from philanthropic or private-sector funders and participate in a third-party evaluation. If the program achieves its targets and generates savings, the government returns a portion of those savings to the funders. In effect, the promise of future savings funds preventive services right now.

This approach to funding resembles investing in a new business. If the business turns a profit, the investments pay off; if not, all or part of the investment is lost—to the investor or philanthropist, but, in this case, not the taxpayer. An especially desirable feature of Pay for Success is that it brings many of the benefits of business investing to government programs: clear goals, important outcome measures to judge success, rigorous evaluations of program outcomes, and pressure on program operators to produce impacts.

To date, several agencies have supported small Pay for Success programs. But there's the potential to do more, especially in the areas of educating young children with disabilities and reducing homelessness. Recently, bipartisan teams in the House and Senate have introduced bills to provide a permanent source of funding for Pay for Success, a $300 million fund based at the Department of the Treasury, which can fund interventions across different agencies.[93] Congress should enact these proposals.

As exciting as Pay for Success is, it is still a new and complex idea, and it can be a poor fit for Washington in cases where federal taxpayer savings do not exist or arise over the very long term. Intervention targeted at young children without special needs, for example, can have long-term effects on education and earnings but probably won't yield rapid financial savings. These long-term outcomes need to be encouraged, especially because they can contribute to restoring America's promise of intergenerational social mobility. The tiered-evidence-based initiatives sometimes create that opportunity, but it's spotty. For example, the Department of Education's Investing in Innovation program began with the idea of "scaling up" what works, but in recent competitions, it has aimed to spread more limited funds across more providers with less evidence. The Social Innovation Fund has similarly focused on funding promising ideas.

For these reasons, we recommend widening the Pay for Success initiative to offer substantial up-front grant funding for the handful of programs that are demonstrated to have a high social return on investment and a large impact on increasing social mobility. Few programs would meet this standard at first, but that is okay. Taxpayers—and the people designing and running good programs—ought to know that money is available to grow extraordinary interventions with extraordinary returns.

Grantees would first need to cross the threshold of having rigorous evidence of a large impact on an important outcome, whether it's getting ready for school or finding a good job or avoiding prison. To permit comparisons across issue areas, from preventing recidivism to encouraging college completion, grantees would be ranked using cost-benefit analysis, and only initiatives with high return on investment would be funded. Funding could be provided in a Pay for Success format, but it would not need to be. Program administration could be consolidated with the new Pay for Success fund proposed at the Department of the Treasury, which would be closely coordinated with poverty-reduction programs at other agencies. Use of intermediaries could be encouraged, but not required as in the Social Innovation Fund, and support could be given to programs that aim to achieve multiple outcomes across a population.

The combination of Pay for Success and scaling "what works" initiatives could generate billions of dollars in new funding for effective interventions. But because those costs are so substantial, we offer proposals for specific funding mechanisms later.

Recommendation 10: Transform existing formula and competitive grants. Our previous three recommendations would expand the most-innovative approaches to funding what works. But these recommendations don't address an even tougher question: What will we do with the great majority of federal grant programs that *don't* require evidence? Unless we improve the way these programs allocate funds, the federal government will continue to waste taxpayer money, and many interventions won't produce the results they could.

Changing core programs—such as the Community Development Block Grant—will take hard work and courage. Programs have built constituencies around one way of doing business. Change will often be unwelcome. But it's necessary.

Different strategies for basing programs on evidence will be appropriate in different cases. In existing competitive grant programs, there should be priorities for grant proposals that bring strong evidence of important successes and that require evaluations. Because running a grant program that evaluates evidence and supports rigorous site-level evaluations is costly, increasing use of evidence will sometimes mean consolidating smaller programs. Such consolidation can not only allow for evidence to influence funding decisions but also eliminate inefficient federal rules that get in the way of the best approaches to problem solving. (See our "lookback" discussion below.)

Promoting the use of evidence in programs that make grants based on a formula (usually related to population) is more complicated. The simplest approach is to require grantees to use a portion of formula funds for interventions proven to be evidence based. But this only works where there are strong, accessible lists of practices that grantees have the ability to use. Congress recently used this approach for mental health block grants.

Another promising strategy is to award a small portion of large formula grants to be awarded competitively based upon grantees' effective use of formula grants—as measured by outcomes, the use of evidence-based practices, or some combination of these metrics. The Bush administration's $10 million home-visiting initiative worked this way. The federal government can also require states and localities to use some formula funds to develop their own capacity for evidence-based decision making. And lastly, when metrics are strong, the federal government can simply require that formula grantees meet baseline performance standards or lose funding.

The ultimate goal is that formula grant programs provide so much support for evidence-based initiatives and their evaluation that many tiered initiatives become unnecessary. Little by little, the evidence-based approach can improve the nation's domestic programs and even lead to continuous improvement through rigorous evaluation. As part of the "lookback" process described below, the next administration should conduct an assessment of major funding streams to determine which strategies to pursue in each context.

Recommendation 11: Conduct a grant-program "lookback" to replace mandates for processes with incentives for outcomes. For many grant programs, simply demanding greater use of evidence and evaluation is not enough. These programs also require all sorts of procedures and services that constrain innovation. At the same time, the programs aren't clear about what they need to accomplish. That structure needs to be reversed.

Consider Head Start, the nation's largest and most important preschool program. In the only large-scale RCT ever performed on Head Start, children who participated in the program saw immediate gains in school readiness, but any advantage appeared to vanish by third grade.[94] Yet other early-childhood programs have stronger outcomes.

Head Start has "performance standards" that run to 145 pages and dictate everything from seating arrangements at lunch to membership on parent councils to timing for parent-teacher conferences.[95] While any one rule is reasonable, the cumulative effect of having so many is to discourage innovation and encourage a culture of box checking instead. Head Start still lacks a clear, manageable list of the skills (cognitive, social, emotional) that the program is supposed to impart and measure. Partly as a result, most programs use curricula that have been shown in research not to drive improved child outcomes.[96]

The people who run Head Start programs are deeply dedicated to children and want to do right by them. And Head Start is improving. It now requires grantees that receive poor ratings to compete to keep their grants. Programs are rated based on expert observations of classrooms, using procedures that have been shown to modestly predict student outcomes. The combination of ratings and "recompetition" represents real progress. But there is a lot of work to do. Even with the competition, most incumbents are keeping their grants—including those who have achieved only mediocre results.

Head Start should develop and implement a set of performance measures that reflect the skills young children need to succeed in school. At the same time, the program should free providers from many of the current performance standards so that they can try different approaches to helping kids learn. The recompetition process should include a broader range of performance measures. And all programs should have new incentives to adopt more evidence-based practices, such as better curricula.

We are confident that these types of reforms would be helpful in a range of federal programs, from Job Corps to college-access initiatives. And the government could use a common process for identifying such reforms. In the regulatory context, OIRA in 2011 led a government-wide regulatory "lookback" process requiring agencies to "reexamine their significant rules and streamline, reduce, improve, or eliminate them on the basis of that examination."[97] The lookback process yielded scores of measures to update regulatory regimes.

Virtually every grant program could use such a lookback as well—a review of all the current rules to see if they have the right balance between mandating a baseline of services supported by evidence and incentivizing excellence. In some cases, legislation would be needed, but in others, regulations could achieve significant reforms. The goal of the lookback process would be to institute stronger performance metrics, incentives, and evaluations; to simplify or eliminate accreted requirements that are no longer useful; and, in some cases, to eliminate small, siloed, and prescriptive programs and replace them with larger, more integrated, and more evidence-based initiatives.

Recommendation 12: Create new flexibility to test new approaches to fighting poverty. Evaluation of state welfare experiments led to the important reforms of the nation's major cash welfare program enacted in 1996. These experiments were made possible by a provision in the Social Security Act allowing the secretary of health and human services to grant waivers that would permit demonstrations designed to promote the purposes of the act. Other major federal social programs should have—and use—similar authorities that encourage experimentation by state and local governments. This would clear the path for new approaches to increasing self-sufficiency and cut poverty.

The problem is that what strikes you as sensible experimentation may strike me as an attack on all that is good in the world. And nobody wants experimentation to be unlimited. But if we are to improve the quality of government, both political parties will need to show greater willingness to err on the side of innovation.

In 2012, President Obama proposed to allow states to change the way they measure the number of people who are engaged in "work-related activities" under welfare. Republicans immediately jumped on this proposal as an attempt to "gut welfare reform." In fact, the proposal would have allowed states to test plausible new ideas for supporting self-sufficiency, such as greater use of subsidized employment. Republicans had previously supported greater flexibility in welfare programs, and for good reason since the program had been created in 1996 based on experiences with waivers in forty states. Still, the administration's announcement just before the election was problematic, and the criticism was intense. In response, the Obama administration made some sensible changes to the proposal, but by this point the issue was so politically toxic that nobody was interested in waivers. That's too bad, and the idea deserves a second look. Waivers from static program rules almost always deserve a second look.

Recently Congressman Paul Ryan proposed what he has called Opportunity Grants. These would allow a handful of states to combine a wide range of both discretionary and entitlement programs, including food stamps, welfare, child care, and housing assistance. Aid recipients would be required to draw up a "life plan" with social-service providers, and able-bodied people would be required to work. States would contract with different organizations that provide services to the poor. The states and the federal government would set benchmarks for outcomes and evaluate the results.

Many progressives have responded to this proposal by focusing on its most controversial component: the elimination of the individual guarantee of the Supplemental Nutrition Assistance Program (SNAP), formerly known as food stamps. And it is fair to ask how this cost-neutral proposal jibes with House Republicans' other proposals to make significant cuts in SNAP and other social programs. Since welfare reform, SNAP represents the country's only commitment to guaranteeing benefits to all poor individuals and families.

Still, as with the Republican response to Obama's waivers, Democrats should not overlook ways in which the Ryan proposal matches ideas of their own. The government's compartmentalization of poverty programs (housing, education, health, etc.) often doesn't match up with real life. A victim of domestic violence may need emergency housing, transportation to school for a child, and mental-health services all at once. She needs an integrated solution, not a jigsaw puzzle with the pieces thrown all over the floor—different programs, eligibility requirements, offices, and so forth.

In the particular context of helping "disconnected youth" (those aged 16–24 and not in school or working), President Obama proposed and Congress recently created an authority for "performance partnerships" that will allow states and localities to pool annually appropriated funds and receive waivers from program-specific requirements in education, training, health, and community-service programs. State or local leaders would propose new metrics for improving outcomes, and results would be evaluated.

Congress should come together behind extending the existing performance-partnership authority into new domains, including programs addressing housing and criminal justice. And while it makes sense for progressives to want to preserve SNAP as an entitlement, the other programs that Ryan proposed to subject to waivers do not currently reach all eligible individuals anyway. With strong protections (including for current recipients of these benefits), Congress should offer more flexibility to a few states over these funds, provided that in return they commit to getting better outcomes, as measured through rigorous evaluation.

Offering more flexibility in exchange for more accountability and evaluation will often be a promising formula, though in some instances it will require new funding in order to work. The recently enacted Farm Bill included $200 million to test out new approaches to providing job training for food-stamp recipients. If these approaches succeed in moving significant numbers of individuals out of poverty, they could save far more than $200 million in a program that cost more than $80 billion in 2013. Because of the evaluations, we'll know.

The same approach could also help strengthen some of America's largest and most important programs. For example, the disability-insurance program within Social Security provides a safety net for millions of Americans who have worked hard during their lives but are no longer able to work due to illness or injury. The program costs more than $140 billion per year, and the share of working-age Americans who are receiving payments has risen substantially over the last three decades, a trend largely but not entirely explained by demographic and economic trends.[98] As Jeff Liebman and Jack Smalligan have shown, there are innovations in the program that might help protect the vulnerable, hold overall costs to current or lower levels, and enable more individuals to stay in the workforce.[99] And the Social Security Administration could be testing these approaches today if it had appropriate authority and funding. Congress should provide them.

Finally, communities could utilize the combination of flexibility and funding to tackle America's most central challenges. Liebman has fleshed out the compelling idea of a "Ten-Year Challenge" that would modestly fund ten communities to seek to achieve break-through results in addressing ten problems over ten years, ranging from recidivism to homelessness, with flexibility as needed across funding streams and an evaluation of the results.[100] State and local governments could achieve a great deal more if they were able to organize their efforts around meeting these ambitious goals, rather than complying with different programmatic requirements.

MOVING FUNDS FROM LESS-EFFECTIVE TO MORE-EFFECTIVE PROGRAMS

Recommendation 13: Offset costs to encourage reforms. Democrats and Republicans disagree about whether to increase domestic spending. So do the two of us. But we both agree that the

Moneyball agenda we have outlined should be implemented even if domestic spending does not increase by one penny.

From a cost perspective, our proposals fall into three categories. First, some recommendations improve existing programs with no new costs. Reforms to existing competitive and formula grant programs and targeted interventions fall into this category.

Second, expanding the federal evaluation infrastructure would have modest costs. If savings to pay for this spending are needed, it is appropriate to create a small levy across entire agencies. The needed reduction in current spending would be very modest. The cross-agency approach avoids creating a line item that budget cutters could foolishly target. It also reflects the reality that evaluation and data systems provide broad benefits for agencies, their programs, and the populations they are supposed to serve.

Third, a few of our recommendations have substantial new costs. Expanding existing evidence based initiatives and creating a "Scale What Works for Social Mobility" program could cost billions, though their social benefits are likely to be much greater. When waivers are granted, testing new approaches (as with disability) can require new up-front funding as well.

There are several options for cuts to pay for this new spending. President Obama's budgets have included several billion dollars in as-yet un-enacted program cuts that could be sources of new resources.[101] These measures range from reductions in spending on oil-and-gas research to reforms and reductions in the Senior Community Service Employment Program.

If these measures are not sufficient, a final good option would be to reduce the largest block-grant programs that currently lack strong evidence criteria. These reductions could be linked to increases in evidence-based initiatives. For example, if the Scale What Works initiative funded a large evidence-based initiative to scale up a proven job-training strategy, the reductions could come from the job-training formula programs. This is not a first choice, because the formula grants ensure at least some level of services across the country, and evidence-based programs will not replace all services in all places that are lost due to cuts. However, evidence-based programs are carefully designed to achieve higher levels of impact than typical block grants. In addition, because of their emphasis on evaluation, these programs can generate learning that is useful across all government programs. Finally, while reductions in block grants will lead to reductions in services in some places, the increases in evidence-based programs will lead to expansions in services in other places. The greater concentration of services in some areas over others is not optimal, but roughly the same number of people would be served as from formula-only programs. The key is that with the evidence-based programs, the average quality of service and their average impacts on social problems will be higher.

CONCLUSION

If you're a member of Congress or an executive-branch official who is looking to allocate scarce dollars, what do you do? Historically, you make changes on the margins. You look at the research and do your best to infer what works, realizing you don't know much. You try to avoid big political problems.

If you're a nonprofit-organization leader looking for government funding, what do you do? Historically, you find someone who knows someone who makes decisions. You get some constituents to lobby on your behalf. You do some polling. These days, maybe you start a social-media campaign.

These are exactly the dynamics that our proposals would change. They create a vibrant marketplace with both supply and demand in what works. They create the supply of what works by funding more evaluations to identify effective interventions. And they create the demand for what works by driving grant dollars toward interventions that work.

In this new era, government officials will have access to rich data and a far better idea of what works. And program leaders will know that in order to get funding, what they will need isn't influence or anecdotes; it's evidence.

And that's what it means to play Moneyball for government.

MONEYBALL LEADERS

Interviews with
- Raj Shah
- Linda Gibbs
- Tiffany Cooper Gueye
- Dan Cardinali
- Yvette Sanchez Fuentes
- Jim Shelton

All around the country, leaders have been leveraging data, evidence, and evaluation to do their jobs better and to make sure the missions of the organizations they lead are met. We sat down with six leaders in a range of fields and asked them each the same five questions. About the particular challenges they faced. About the obstacles they overcame. And about advice they could give others who are ready to embark on a Moneyball mission of their own.

What follows are lightly edited transcripts of those interviews.

INTERVIEW WITH RAJ SHAH

Raj Shah has served as administrator at the U.S. Agency for International Development since 2009.

BRIEFLY DESCRIBE THE ORGANIZATIONAL CHANGE YOU LED THAT RESULTED IN YOUR ORGANIZATION EMBRACING AN "INVEST IN WHAT WORKS" APPROACH. DID IT WORK?

When I started, the first few months of my role were really consumed by the Haiti earthquake response. This was *the* largest natural disaster, most catastrophic ever experienced, two hours from Miami. And at USAID, we were very hands-on in handling a massive whole-of-government response. And what became clear on day one or day two was that the government was set up to do a very effective job of describing the process of what we were doing but was not as naturally set up to track and to define the full extent of the needs and then describe in a metrics-based way the percentage of the need we were filling and what the gap was. We wanted to be able to focus on the gaps and solve problems as opposed to just doing more of the same and calling it success.

So, early on in that response, we did a lot of things that, frankly, I didn't at the time even really perceive as innovative. We created a data system that would allow us to say, "Okay. We estimate three million people need food and water, and we have provided X amount of commodities and Y number of flights and distributed all those items to twenty-two NGOs. And through all of that effort, we've reached twelve percent of the total three million people who are in need. So how do we get from twelve to eighty or eighty-five?"

That kind of metrics-based approach to tracking the results from the Haiti earthquake response allowed us to do some things differently in that context. It liberated a lot of these supercreative, very, very talented disaster response specialists to say, "Oh, hey, in the tsunami we tried this" or "If we're not really reaching enough of the children who are in the camps around Port-au-Prince, we can try these sets of things." We would then track after the fact the results they were actually achieving as opposed to up front requiring them to detail out, for example, all of the process protections they'd put into place to make sure the food wasn't stolen.

At the end of that, we looked back and thought we had a pretty successful initial response that exceeded many people's belief about how quickly we could mobilize this global and interagency effort. So that kind of data-driven approach and mind-set, which was relatively easier to execute in the context of a full-on crisis, then became the basis for a set of reforms we called USAID Forward, and that's really the second element of the institutional change.

We launched USAID Forward in April of that year, and it was basically an effort to rebuild an agency that had over time lost more than 40 percent of its staffing, its policy and analysis capabilities, and its accountability for running its own budget. Frankly, we were doing a lot of monitoring process but very little real impact evaluation on what was transpiring, so it was important to me that we reinvest in training our people around evidence-based decision making. So that was really the start of a major reform effort that continues to this day.

There's a book about Alan Mulally, who was the CEO of Ford Motor Company, called *American Icon*, which is about how he really turned around Ford Motor Company not by making huge staffing changes but by changing the culture and the focus on evidence-based decision making and a culture of helping each other out instead of fighting each other inside the management team.

To this day, people make fun of me for the extent to which I've adopted that book and Alan's business process as our management approach. We put in place our version of something called the "business process review," which is a very strict process he uses to have evidence-based management at Ford. And so basically every month or every six weeks we sit down and every business unit reports on their five objectives. They describe their performances in three colors—red, yellow, or green—based on actual data on performance. And, where they have yellows and reds, they ask their colleagues for help because a lot of the yellows and reds can be turned around by other people's experience or because something's stuck in some other person's part of the organization, and it has allowed over the course of two years for a much more data-driven management system.

And in fact we've now increased our performance on a federal survey of evidence-based decision making: we are fifth out of twenty-four federal agencies. I credit a lot of our ongoing ability to be evidence driven and to implement those reforms to that management approach.

Let me give you a sense of how this kind of evidence-based focus can really produce results. One really instructive example is our effort in child survival. The United States is the largest funder of efforts to save children's lives around the world in poor communities. And we spend around $1.5 billion to $2 billion a year on that task. We were trying to ask ourselves, "Are we driving these resources toward those efforts that will give us the most actual lives saved per dollar year after year?" Our desire is, of course, to save as many children as humanly possible with the money we have.

What we found from some visits and some early analysis was that, perhaps, too much of that money was being spent by contractors and grantees in Washington on expenses driven in the Beltway, which obviously is not saving lives in-country. And then when you looked in-country, too much of that money was spent duplicating systems as opposed to driving results. So our malaria program would have its own procurement and supply chain for malaria drugs, and a vaccine-delivery program would have its own procurement and supply chain for vaccines. And you could literally go to countries and see warehouses across the street from each other that were built, one for the malaria-control effort and one for a series of other disease-control efforts—HIV, for example.

So we said, "Well, this doesn't feel like the most efficient way to spend." But we also didn't want to create a perception that we're using money inefficiently, especially because on the whole this program has been one of the big success stories over twenty years. You've seen massive reductions in child deaths, from 12.6 million kids dying under the age of five in 1990 to 6.6 million in 2013. So we didn't want to disparage the program, but we wanted it to get better.

So we brought an outside group of experts together led by Ray Chambers, who is a successful business leader in New York. And then he built a group that includes political leaders like Harris Wofford and philanthropists like Jean Case, some procurement specialists, a couple of private-equity guys who buy companies and then drive process improvements in the companies. And then the Gates Foundation joined and gave us a grant to use consultants to help with the effort.

But it was mostly internally driven. We built a team across our management functions and our global-health functions and the twenty-four missions where 70 percent of the children who die by the age of five die every year. Over the course of a year and a half we went through every grant, every contract, every project, identified the major areas where we could make a more evidence-based shift of resources to save more children's lives. And in June 2014 we were able to publish the results of all that work, which was that we can basically reallocate $2.9 billion over two years to save five hundred thousand additional child lives. And I'm beyond excited about that because I've been to the projects, and I know we've gone in very, very deep on the process. And aside from just saving more children's lives, which is obviously a tremendous moral win, it has changed this project, and the process has very much changed the kind of culture and mind-set of our health officers in the field, where they're not just saying, "Okay, this is how we do something." Instead they're saying, "Is this the best way to save the most children's lives?" And given how talented those folks are, country after country, getting them asking the right questions and presenting data to justify that, I think, is transforming this field. This is a really, really fundamental shift in mind-set, and I personally believe it's going to be one of the real lasting contributions that our health team has made to the world.

WHY DID YOU EMBRACE A MONEYBALL APPROACH, AND WHAT WERE YOUR BIGGEST CONCERNS BEFORE YOU GOT STARTED?

Well, I think the big motivating factor is that development is just too important for our nation's foreign policy and national security to be spending resources and not being able to articulate what the results are and whether we're delivering the most value for dollars that we're spending. And USAID has had this amazing legacy and history of doing some breakthrough things, like powering the green revolution that helped hundreds of millions of people avoid starvation in the 1970s and 1980s and inventing new health strategies, like oral-rehydration solution that saved millions of children's lives in the 1980s and 1990s.

But too often we rely on just a couple of successful examples and not a more comprehensive ability to say, "Are we optimizing across our total portfolio in terms of our mission, which is to move people out of extreme poverty and reduce, as much as possible, child death and child hunger?" So that was the motivation.

The biggest concern was really whether we had capacity to do it. A lot of people said, "You can take this approach at the Gates Foundation, but you can't take it here because Congress won't let you" or "If you admit that you're spending the child-survival resources in a nonoptimal way, which the very process of trying to implement this results-oriented approach would validate, then you'll get your budget cut and you'll expose the administration to a strong critique from Congress."

Another concern was about size. We have 9,600 employees across more than seventy countries, so we're a big, distributed organization. And people said, "You won't be able to bring the teams together across such a decentralized institution to get this done." And yet another, which is probably the most true, said that many of the contract partners won't go for this. And, in fact, when we started, we tried things like placing more emphasis on cost by requiring contractors to propose in a manner we believed would show value for money and cost-effectiveness. Some of our external partners protested that. It was news to me that, in the federal-procurement system, that's a valid lawsuit, but nevertheless, it was a little surprising to me that not everybody had that same motivation of just optimizing results for what we were spending.

WHAT WAS YOUR TOUGHEST OBSTACLE IN GETTING YOUR ORGANIZATION TO EMBRACE THIS APPROACH?

The biggest thing was just getting the culture of the agency to embrace trying something new. There are just so many reasons why something can't be done, or it doesn't work this way, or we need to water down our approach because of Congress or regulations or this rule, or the State Department won't like it, or you're exposing the White House to a bad press story if it's told the wrong way. Changing that internal instinct to avoid risk was probably the single biggest obstacle.

And part of how we overcame that obstacle was using a lot of external partners to help us think differently. But it was also about bringing our internal team into the process, sharing a ton of data with them, and showing them where we're weak and can get better. Seeing it like that really forces you to fully live up to your aspiration.

Even when we saved the $2.9 billion, this could have been an issue. We could have stayed very general, not made any reference to the $2.9 billion because everybody was very nervous that Congress would say, "Oh, if you have that volume of resourcing that you think you can reallocate from low-productive use to high-productive use, then you have too much money, and we're going to take some away."

So I think that instinct was the biggest challenge. And the way we overcame it was just bringing external partners in to help keep us focused and insist from us that we make the tough decisions and take the risks because, once they've invested their effort and energy, especially a very high-level outside group, then you have to see it through. They also gave me more courage to be able to know that if something was perceived the wrong way externally, that we have this group of ten or twelve really unimpeachable leaders that could speak to Congress or to others or the press and validate our approach.

WHAT ARE YOUR TOP THREE KEY INSIGHTS OR LESSONS LEARNED?

I think the first is that really very central businesslike or private-sector principles are applicable to and, in fact, important to how public institutions run. As Alan Mulally says in his book over and over, you can't improve something you cannot measure and report on in a quantitative way. That central insight has been the driver of our effort in health, our effort in food security, and so many other things we do. Quantitative, private-sector management principles are very applicable to public management.

A second insight is about risk taking. That it's not really just about a few exceptional people doing something extraordinary but rather creating a collaborative environment that allows for real risk taking, where people believe, if we all collectively are cognizant of those risks and we have strategies in place, we can manage those risks effectively. And really instilling that collaborative culture takes a long, long time. I don't actually think it can be done in six months or eight months.

And really it's hard to articulate how nervous the best, most talented, most committed global experts were about doing this work. I mean it really felt like we were violating procurement rules, which we were not. They felt we were exposing ourselves to congressional critique. But at the end of the day we were applauded, not cut. They thought that in a complex interagency environment, this would lower our standing. They didn't think we had the time or data to do this, and it turns out they figured out how to make the time and how to find the data to do it. They thought our partners would revolt or be very challenging, and then they were the ones who brought our partners to the table in a way where it was a real collaboration. So it really is building a culture that allows for the risk taking.

My last insight is that when we take this kind of an approach, we can actually dramatically build political support for our efforts. And folks find it hard to believe, but I think because we're doing these types of things, Congress has actually increased our budget. In fact, fiscal year 2013 is my favorite year because, despite sequestration when everybody else got cut, our core accounts actually went up even more than President Obama asked for in his budget because of this unique collaboration between Republicans and Democrats. And when they did it, they were very clear. They were doing it because they believed in this approach. They didn't think enough people in government were taking these kinds of approaches, and they wanted us to have a chance at being successful.

WHAT ADVICE DO YOU HAVE FOR OTHERS?

I think part of it is, leaders—especially in the public arena—have to have extraordinary conviction to see it through because the reasons to not do it and the concern about taking risks are so deeply held and so deeply felt. You must have a tremendous amount of conviction to see it through. And frankly, I've gotten some of that conviction from external friends and colleagues who came together on these various advisory boards and spent time digging deep into our work and meeting our teams and being involved. Without that external sounding board, I would have, in many cases, probably failed to go as far as we've been able to go.

INTERVIEW WITH LINDA GIBBS

Linda Gibbs was deputy mayor of New York City for health and human services from 2005 to 2013, where she founded the Center for Economic Opportunity.

BRIEFLY DESCRIBE THE ORGANIZATIONAL CHANGE YOU LED THAT RESULTED IN YOUR ORGANIZATION EMBRACING AN "INVEST IN WHAT WORKS" APPROACH. DID IT WORK?

The most formative experience for me on this was in 1996, when we were creating a new child-welfare agency in New York City, born out of a tragic child fatality that uncovered a totally dysfunctional child-welfare system—from inattention to reports of abuse, to failure to monitor how well children were served by providers. We introduced the use of data to bring better accountability and improved outcomes to the foster-care system for the first time. We hardwired these outcomes into service contracts with providers in a way that drove attention and created consequences based on the actual performance.

If you can get your program outcomes measured and aligned to the ultimate values and goals you bring to the table, that ability to measure and give that feedback to providers about how well they're doing is the most powerful way to move programs more closely to the goals.

The power it had to transform frontline practice and to bring everybody's attention—from the government managers to the non-profit agencies to the external oversight organizations—into clear focus around achieving the goals that were embedded in those outcomes was inspiring. It proved to me that the hard work of aligning values, goals, and outcomes is key to improving services.

WHY DID YOU EMBRACE A MONEYBALL APPROACH, AND WHAT WERE YOUR BIGGEST CONCERNS BEFORE YOU GOT STARTED?

My child-welfare experience was proof to me that this was an approach that would almost be irresponsible if I didn't continue to use. That experience carried through to other areas of child-welfare practice—making the preventive world more accountable—then into homeless services, both in terms of the effectiveness of homeless prevention and in shelter services.

When I moved to city hall as the deputy mayor and Mayor Bloomberg engaged me in a conversation around really wanting to understand what is causing so many people to be stuck in poverty, I was able to bring this experience with me to try to answer the mayor's questions.

While the child-welfare work was to apply those Moneyball principles to an existing set of practices in order to discern the different levels of outcomes providers were producing to distinguish the stronger ones from the weaker ones, the mayor's question was, how were we going to test and evaluate new solutions? We have all these great ideas of things that we think are going to have a big impact on changing people's lives in poverty. But in many ways, many of them were untested. And so we structured the entire Center for Economic Opportunity initiative around having a very strong evaluation metric so that as these new things were tested, we'd be able to distinguish those that were, in fact, having their intended effect from those that were a perfectly good idea but didn't work out for any variety of reasons. And so that was the real metamorphosis of the Moneyball approach in my New York City government experience.

WHAT WAS YOUR TOUGHEST OBSTACLE IN GETTING YOUR ORGANIZATION TO EMBRACE THIS APPROACH?

Initially, the biggest obstacles were the nonprofit providers and the government-program people, who were very invested in their current programs and felt very strongly that they knew what the best things were and didn't want to really upset the applecart, and perhaps were a little bit afraid of the results that they were going to see once the evaluations came back. So just dealing with all of that resistance was a huge barrier.

A second and incredibly significant barrier is just the ability to manage data effectively. If you are going to create consequences around the results that get reported, your data systems had better be right. And you're dealing with legacy systems that have a ton of dirty data. When it didn't count for anything, nobody would be that concerned about what data they're inputting. And suddenly when it starts to count either in terms of consequences for contracts or continuation of programs, or ultimately for the quality of the services that are being delivered to real people, you'd better be really confident that your data systems are accurate. So that was a huge concern as well.

And then ultimately, if you do it, there are going to be consequences. And people fear having a mirror back on them of the quality of their work for the first time after, in some cases, decades of doing the work. To expose yourself to that kind of accountability with data feedback is a high-risk proposition that people just were not accustomed to. So changing the culture to make people more comfortable with that data feedback and developing systems to make sure that there is a learning process and that it wasn't punitive was a huge obstacle as well.

WHAT ARE YOUR TOP THREE KEY INSIGHTS OR LESSONS LEARNED?

I think it's critical to develop outcome measures that are very tightly aligned to your high-level goals for your system management or reform. It's a hugely powerful communications tool. People will read your speeches and your press releases until the cows come home. But then they'll just put them in their circular file. If you embed an outcome measure in how they are evaluated, they are going to focus on that with great intensity. And they're going to think hard about what's going to produce the outcome you want to achieve. And so the first lesson is to really work hard, to make sure that you are not wasting a single opportunity to create those outcomes that align with your key programmatic goals. It is also important to do it in a simple way, asking, what are the top five outcomes, and then really getting people to concentrate their efforts around those key values. That is, by far, the most important step.

The second is to help people get comfortable with the data: clean up the dirty data, but also just give people a chance to work with it. A lot of times, people haven't had the opportunity to even know the consequences of what they're doing because there has been no data feedback loop. Government is famous for data in, data in, data in, but never giving any data back out to let people know the knowledge that has been accumulated. So spend time to invest in bringing the whole system along in understanding the data and the data-management practices. And when the data is clean and accurate, give people a chance to live with the results for a little bit before you tie consequences to those results so that they can be less fearful of the information they're going to get and more responsive in how to adjust their practices to produce the kind of outcomes that you want.

But then ultimately, when all of that is ripe, there really needs to be consequences. You can't just feed data out and say, "And by the way, one-third of the system is performing extraordinarily poorly for children and families," and have no consequence for that. You need to create very concrete consequences in performance-based contracts, where those who do well are rewarded with either higher rates or a greater share of the work, and those who do poorly have consequences for that. Because ultimately, if there's not a consequence, then the data won't matter one bit, and people won't take it seriously.

WHAT ADVICE DO YOU HAVE FOR OTHERS?

Do not be fearful of this. I think that there are so many concerns: Will I get it? Will I design it right? Will I do it right? Will my front-line staff manage it right? And there are so many fears about the risks that are involved in this transition. Ultimately, the bottom-line advice is to not be fearful, because by not delving in and doing it, you're depriving yourself of an incredibly powerful tool that can help you get where you want your system to go much more cleanly, quickly, and effectively than without it.

INTERVIEW WITH TIFFANY COOPER GUEYE

Tiffany Cooper Gueye is the CEO of Building Educated Leaders for Life (BELL), an organization dedicated to providing high-quality after-school and summer learning experiences for high-risk students.

BRIEFLY DESCRIBE THE ORGANIZATIONAL CHANGE YOU LED THAT RESULTED IN YOUR ORGANIZATION EMBRACING AN "INVEST IN WHAT WORKS" APPROACH. DID IT WORK?

We serve K–8 children attending high-poverty, low-performing schools, typically in urban settings. We currently work across nineteen communities in the United States, and we've demonstrated time and again that low-income students who are lagging in school performance actually can do better in school and find a path to reaching their aspirations.

Our theory of change is that if we pull the lever of "time outside of school"—if we provide students with high-quality after-school and summer learning experiences that are academically rigorous, that include parental engagement, and that are enriching—then disadvantaged youth can do better in school, raise their aspirations, and leverage those assets to find a pathway out of poverty. So at a very basic level, we embrace an "invest in what works" approach because we think it's generating an outcome that has importance and value for a set of kids that we believe in.

We've done one independent randomized controlled trial, and we have a second under way. But we've invested in measurement, evaluation, and impact-type activities probably for about sixteen years. Because we have a long history and a culture of learning at BELL, it wasn't really a hard sell getting the organization on board with an "invest in what works" approach. It's something that reflects our commitment to knowing whether our efforts are moving the needle.

I would say the one thing that was a tough sell for the organization that did require some organizational change management was convincing the organization to do a second randomized controlled trial. RCTs are rigorous—and they feel rigorous, too—so they can be intrusive to the organization's operations. RCTs require our operating team to reengineer the enrollment process for our programs—to use a lottery system, for example—and to recruit parents' participation in the study so that we have proper consents. So it's really intensive work. Doing it well requires the buy-in and effectiveness of a staff that was hired to deliver outcomes for kids but not necessarily to measure outcomes for kids. Convincing our team to do a second randomized controlled trial was, perhaps, the one place where there was some change management to be done.

WHY DID YOU EMBRACE A MONEYBALL APPROACH, AND WHAT WERE YOUR BIGGEST CONCERNS BEFORE YOU GOT STARTED?

We embraced a Moneyball approach because too often we see resources being deployed in communities for things that we don't think make a meaningful difference for the children and families being served. And when that happens, it obviously gets in the way of things that are more effective. So a Moneyball approach was something we embraced because we wanted to see greater results generated when resources are allocated, and it's just not happening enough right now in our sector.

Of course a big fear before we got started—and still remains so—has been that one data point will be used in a black-white way. Something either works or it doesn't work. Instead, a Moneyball approach has to be about using a range of data to help inform resource-allocation decisions.

WHAT WAS YOUR TOUGHEST OBSTACLE IN GETTING YOUR ORGANIZATION TO EMBRACE THIS APPROACH?

There are two things that I think are just the toughest obstacles: One is the cost. Evaluation work involves costs above and beyond program implementation. And if you want great evidence right now, you have to pay a lot of money for it. Relatedly, too few organizations can afford rigorous studies, so when BELL and others can manage to make the investment, there is still not enough collective evidence about the impact of a strategy.

The second toughest obstacle has been the additional recruiting that's required. So imagine the team that works at BELL in my organization and on our board of directors: everybody here is on board and committed to having a Moneyball approach to doing rigorous studies and to facing up to the decisions that come afterward. But there are a bunch of other stakeholders that need to be recruited for this game, and they include the actual beneficiaries— the families that we serve. We have to do the work to help them understand why we'd be taking a Moneyball approach and why we need them to participate in studies. We have partner organizations that we work with that have to be game for this as well. And then the funders. The people that financially support our work, government and private, have to be willing to make the investment and to take on the risk.

WHAT ARE YOUR TOP THREE KEY INSIGHTS OR LESSONS LEARNED?

Defining good evidence is hard. That's my first. There are different types of evidence on the spectrum of rigor, and there are numerous methodological choices an organization or research firm could make. And most important on the spectrum is the fact that there is such a thing as the right study for the right program at the right time in the right organization's life cycle. There's not just one thing that makes sense as a study approach, but it is very specific to where that organization is, where that program is in its life cycle, and the questions that are most valuable to answer. And all of that is to say, there is temptation to simplify how we define "what works" in order for Moneyball to be adopted. But the complexity of it is very appropriate, and we have to maintain that.

As a second insight I would say that even when we are successful generating good evidence, the story of what works is still incomplete. Even when we have well-conducted, highly rigorous studies, there are still limitations in what they tell us about the real nature of social problems, interventions, and changes in the lives of those we reach. As an example, even when randomized controlled trials tell us the story of an organization's work at one point in time, five years later most organizations' work has evolved. So at its best, good evidence is still incomplete.

And then the third insight is that obtaining evidence is risky. Playing Moneyball is a logical and compelling approach to allocating resources. It'll mean good things for kids and families at the other end of this movement, and that, I think, we can all agree to. But there is quite a bit of risk involved. We have to have the right rewards and consequences in place so that positive evidence of impact is viewed in the context of other factors, and less-positive evidence isn't unfairly punished. So you do a randomized controlled trial, and it says your program works. It's not the end of the story. It worked for some group of kids in some context at some point in time, and so we should celebrate that and make sure that's understood. And your randomized-controlled-trial study two years later might say, "It doesn't work for kids or families." And so there, too, we don't want to unfairly punish an organization without understanding that in context. So this risk, I think, is something we'll have to pay more attention to across sectors.

WHAT ADVICE DO YOU HAVE FOR OTHERS?

First, we need better definitions. We need to help outline the array of evidence choices to be made (maintaining the appropriate complexity I spoke to earlier) and even defining what constitutes good outcomes. And I think this will be especially challenging to gain consensus on—in working with a group of third graders to help close the achievement gap, is a good outcome test-score improvement by ten points? Or is it good only if you move test scores by a hundred points? We also need to ensure that evidence and outcomes stay in the context of the kids and the organization.

A second piece of advice would be for regional, private philanthropies to think about their role in Moneyball efforts critically. Getting government to play Moneyball is an appropriate first place to start. But I think we also need to look to local private donors because, at the end of the day, they are going to be the ones that serve to sustain what works in local communities for real kids and families. We need local philanthropies to stop the disruptive work that's going on right now that has funding allocated to things that really aren't quality or moving the needle for kids. If we make a lot of progress nationally, but local philanthropies are still funding their favorite programs that they've funded for the last twenty years, then nothing will change.

And the final piece of advice is to be really clear about what we want in a Moneyball approach and incentivize that. I think we want programs "that work" to grow and reach more beneficiaries. But we also need to create a space that isn't so black-and-white—it worked or didn't work. If we do, organizations will only do the safe studies to minimize their risks. This might be done at the detriment of maximizing their learning.

I believe what we really want is for organizations to be "learning organizations," to ask the right questions, and importantly, to ask the tough questions and not be afraid of what the answer's going to be. I think it's only when we ask the tough questions and we take the risks that our research will actually generate the kind of knowledge that helps us better serve kids and families and actually change their outcomes. Then we are in the best possible position to grow and reach more beneficiaries. So that's all to say we're not just trying to secure resources to sustain and grow what works. We're also trying to actually put forth the interventions that will have the greatest possible impact on our social challenges.

INTERVIEW WITH DAN CARDINALI

Dan Cardinali is the president of Communities in Schools, an organization dedicated to helping students achieve in school, graduate, and go on to bright futures.

BRIEFLY DESCRIBE THE ORGANIZATIONAL CHANGE YOU LED THAT RESULTED IN YOUR ORGANIZATION EMBRACING AN "INVEST IN WHAT WORKS" APPROACH. DID IT WORK?

I've been with the organization for fifteen years, and when I first arrived, we were at a point where we had really grown and scaled immensely quickly. We were up to about 650,000 students after about twenty years, and there'd been a real emphasis on growth for growth's sake. And, as I came in, I was concerned about the quality of our work. I traveled around our network. We had about fourteen local affiliates, all independent 501(c)(3)s, that carry our name and our core work.

But there was a great diffusion of what folks were doing, and there was a saying we had that "If you've seen one Communities in Schools, you've seen one Communities in Schools." So we began a slow but intentional process of building the organization's capacity to really understand what it was doing, whether what it was doing was effective, and then ultimately, building a culture of quality improvement. We began to establish what has become our virtuous learning cycle.

We started with establishing a general identity for the work, and we began to focus around what we called student supports or integrated student supports. We then, over a number of years, put in a performance-management system. The private sector helped us develop that in the late 1990s and early part of the 2000s. And over the course of a number of years, we've compiled a set of results and gotten our entire network working to monitor the same set of indicators. They could do lots of other stuff, but everybody had to follow six key indicators: attendance, behavior, academic course performance, improving promotion rates, lowering dropout rates, and improving graduation rates. This process created a very important foundation of a common identity and enabled folks to learn from each other. There was, in a sense, a common, results-based operating system that began to emerge in the network.

Once we'd established that over a number of years, we were able to develop a five-year, longitudinal-evaluation research design. What was critical about that process is that we included leaders from our network in the design of the third-party evaluation. And so they were able to introduce the nuances and the complexities of the organization so that the design captures the work accurately. In addition, we included a design and implementation evaluation. This was critical because it enabled us to understand what we were doing when we produced results, or not. So that lasted from 2005 into 2010.

Our third-party evaluation was actually a series of eleven different studies, and through the course of it we were able to have a very acute understanding of what we were doing well and what we were not. And every year or sometimes twice yearly, we had a network evaluation committee that was composed of practitioners from our network and outside experts to review the results from the third-party evaluation. So there was co-learning through the process and guidance and really parsing what we were learning and deploying the third-party evaluator to do further analyses so we really could understand. The process was one of the most powerful learning experiences we had ever undertaken.

By the end of the third-party evaluation, we had built internal momentum with this virtuous learning cycle. The data was your friend. It was sometimes very difficult to confront, but it was critical if you wanted to improve and do right by the students and families that we serve. Over time, the virtuous learning cycle was a kind of muscle that got built. It built our capacity to drive fundamental change in our organization. There was both clarity of purpose and a pathway to achieving that purpose.

So that was the first of our two phases. The last phase was a very challenging phase, and that was to take the learnings from the third-party evaluation and build what we called the Total Quality System, a network-wide quality-improvement initiative. TQS was the culmination of the learning gleaned from our performance-management system that was established in the early part of 2000, learning from the third-party evaluation and the practical wisdom of network practitioners. The TQS established a national accreditation process, which we've implemented over the last four years. It means that the learnings from the third-party evaluation and from our own performance-management system were baked into an accreditation process that our entire network had to go through. TQS required the network to implement programmatic work that was validated from the third-party evaluation and we knew was effective. Within a year we'll finish that process. And I'm happy to say that our entire network will have gone through the process, or they will no longer be a part of the network.

Did it work? We won't know for another six months. We have another third-party evaluation specifically set up to test whether the quality-improvement campaign actually was effective. So we should know sometime in the fall of 2015.

WHY DID YOU EMBRACE A MONEYBALL APPROACH, AND WHAT WERE YOUR BIGGEST CONCERNS BEFORE YOU GOT STARTED?

The reason we did it was very, very simple: it was clear to us that our performance-management system was telling us things were going well, but it was inside baseball. We had actually hired a third-party evaluator to evaluate our data-collection system, so we knew it was a solid system, but it didn't seem to have any kind of credibility, to be honest. We would go to outside stakeholders and to our own board. They'd say, "This is great, but how do you know that you're just not cooking the books?"

That was number one. And the second reason was our public accountability. We are a large institution. At that point, when we embarked on this we were working with 650,000 kids. We were taking millions of dollars of public money. Quite frankly, I felt it was the national office's responsibility to be accountable, and I felt an obligation to really know whether we were stewarding those resources well.

And the third reason is a moral obligation. We're about helping poor kids. None of us would send our kids to a doctor that wasn't certified, and so we went out to find out whether we were effective, and we used third-party evaluation to be able to do that.

The biggest concern is, of course, terror: you're terrified when you hire a third-party evaluator that they're going to find something that shows that not only are you not being effective but you're actually doing harm to kids. It was a legitimate fear.

The magnitude of our organization and the complexity of it made it a particularly difficult challenge to figure out a really appropriate research design that would meet nationally rigorous standards and be constructive for our own learning.

And then there is a really fundamental anxiety about our leaders, staff, board members, and volunteers. Our organization attracts—and we intentionally do this—individuals who really love young kids. And when they hear about a third-party evaluator quantifying the impact of love in kids' lives, that's a very difficult proposition. And just remember that even though we have about 4,000 staff, we have about 50,000 to 60,000 volunteers a year. So the vast majority of our workforce are people who do this purely out of goodwill. So there was a very important risk that we had to manage around perception of our organization if this came back negatively.

WHAT WAS YOUR TOUGHEST OBSTACLE IN GETTING YOUR ORGANIZATION TO EMBRACE THIS APPROACH?

The single biggest obstacle we faced wasn't undergoing the third-party evaluation. It was taking the results of it seriously and doing the hard work to change our practice to uniformly become an organization committed to what we knew to be, from that evaluation, the most effective practice. It required substantial change. Everyone believes they're doing great work, and they want the evaluation to merely validate this fact. With great evaluation results, everyone hopes that they'll then get more money so they can continue doing what they're doing. The hard part was when we realized about half our network was doing subpar work, we knew we had to lead a massive quality-improvement campaign.

So in all honesty, despite the really well-trained people here, including myself, we very much blew the change-management strategy, which we started in 2009. We had to reset and restart in 2010. I think the biggest thing we learned is we had to go out to the network and communicate and communicate and communicate. That was number one. And number two is we absolutely had to incentivize folks. Everyone wants quality, but often people are not willing to invest in it. So nationally we ran a $75 million growth-capital campaign. The single biggest investment we made was to reinvest in our network's capacity building. Over the last three years, we've invested north of $30 million to build the capacity of the local affiliates to transition into higher-quality work.

WHAT ARE YOUR TOP THREE KEY INSIGHTS OR LESSONS LEARNED?

First, in the social sector, when you evaluate, you have to manage the fact that you're evaluating not just effective interventions or preventions but also the expression of people's values, which, in our business, is critically important. And that needs to be managed thoughtfully and respectfully.

Number two, you have to provide capacity, support, coaching, and incentives to really help folks change behavior.

And number three, you need to give feedback on the implications of the changed behavior. It's not enough to say, "Good for you." It's "What difference did it make in the expression of the very values you've now brought into question for folks?"

I'll give an example. After the first year and a half of running this quality-improvement campaign, we ran an evaluation of the sites that we had accredited. We were able to show other affiliates that the accredited sites were able to get better outcomes while serving more kids. This sends a really strong message for other affiliates to go through the same process.

WHAT ADVICE DO YOU HAVE FOR OTHERS?

I think the single biggest piece of advice is to pivot to an evidence-based way of proceeding. And I think at the heart of it is this notion of committing to virtuous learning—to always embedding in your professional life, in your organization's life, in your programmatic work, a clear sense of what you are doing; to rigorously determining your effectiveness; gleaning all you can learn from your work; and constantly improving your work. Then repeating the cycle.

The good news is that once that cycle gets unleashed, it just keeps you moving. You get more sophisticated. You learn about implementation. You learn more-effective evaluation strategies for your particular work. You create a community of practitioners who begin to embrace this and become innovative in the process. And it becomes a very powerful virtuous dynamic. But I think at the heart of it is stepping into a different way of proceeding.

INTERVIEW WITH YVETTE SANCHEZ FUENTES

From 2009 to 2013, **Yvette Sanchez Fuentes** *served as director of the Office of Head Start.*

BRIEFLY DESCRIBE THE ORGANIZATIONAL CHANGE YOU LED THAT RESULTED IN YOUR ORGANIZATION EMBRACING AN "INVEST IN WHAT WORKS" APPROACH. DID IT WORK?

While I was at the Office of Head Start within the Department of Health and Human Services, our view was that everyone's opinion mattered. And by that I mean there was a lot of expertise based on experience. And so one example of that would be that we often would come up with approaches that we thought were innovative and new, and when you looked around the organization within the Office of Head Start, you'd find that a lot of the approaches that we were coming up with were things that had been done in the past.

So as we tried to figure out what had worked in the past, we really took those activities, analyzed them for what they had been, what they had done, and then tried to tweak them in a way that would work for Head Start grantees today in 2014. And then the other piece along the way that we added was ensuring that we were collecting data so that we could really take the time to figure out if things were working.

Did it work? That, I think, remains to be seen. I think for a lot of folks who have been in government or worked with local, state, or federal government, what you'll find is that it takes a long time for things to go through the entire process. I think over the next couple of years we'll be able to see whether some of the approaches that I started have really changed the way that local programs organize and align their practices toward serving kids and families.

WHY DID YOU EMBRACE A MONEYBALL APPROACH, AND WHAT WERE YOUR BIGGEST CONCERNS BEFORE YOU GOT STARTED?

We decided to embrace a Moneyball approach because we knew that in order to make change in what local organizations or grantees were doing, we had to have the data, and so we had to be able to tell programs what works and what doesn't work. And in some areas that happened fairly quickly. In others, we still don't really know what works and what doesn't. So the folks who are still at the Office of Head Start are continuing in that same vein, trying to figure out, first of all, what are the data questions that you should be asking, what's the data that you should be collecting, and for what purpose? And then how do you analyze that data in order to help local programs do the best job that they can?

WHAT WAS YOUR TOUGHEST OBSTACLE IN GETTING YOUR ORGANIZATION TO EMBRACE THIS APPROACH?

Within the Office of Head Start it wasn't very tough to get folks to embrace the approach. The toughest part is really trying to figure out what type of data you should be collecting and for what purposes. And most folks who understand Head Start will tell you that Head Start collects a lot, a lot, a lot of data to try to make decisions. But the biggest challenge has always been what you do with all of that. And so within the Office of Head Start, we really had to take a step back and think about key questions: What are the basic things that we want to know? What information do we need in order to then convince grantees and convince other organizations that this is the right approach to be taking?

WHAT ARE YOUR TOP THREE KEY INSIGHTS OR LESSONS LEARNED?

I have one very broad lesson learned, and that's that as we think about evidence-based approaches, there has to be some space for thinking about and including promising practices. And so the biggest lesson that I learned while being in the government and now moving outside of government is that we really have to think about an infrastructure all the way from Congress to the executive branch to research institutions to think tanks to local practitioners so that we have what we need to tell us what we already know works, which is the evidence-based approach, but we also support those promising practices.

So if you are in a local community and you have a community-based organization that has been providing services for five years or for decades, as we have in this country, those organizations have some support and some technical assistance to figure out what's working and what's not working in the way that they do their job. And so I would say that that's the one thing I learned about what's missing. There needs to be some space there for some flexibility, for some promising practices, for taking into account the cultural pieces that happen within communities.

WHAT ADVICE DO YOU HAVE FOR OTHERS?

So the one piece of advice I have is to communicate often. But that isn't just about the government doing a better job of communicating to the public. It's about, within the government, constantly sharing information about what you're doing, why you're doing it, and what the goal is. This is the only way to make sure you are bringing those folks along with you who are going to be there long after you leave so that they can continue to implement this change, and it really becomes something that's institutionalized rather than something that's just the latest fad, depending on who is in that position of power.

INTERVIEW WITH JIM SHELTON

Jim Shelton is the deputy secretary at the U.S. Department of Education.

BRIEFLY DESCRIBE THE ORGANIZATIONAL CHANGE YOU LED THAT RESULTED IN YOUR ORGANIZATION EMBRACING AN "INVEST IN WHAT WORKS" APPROACH. DID IT WORK?

As the head of the Office of Innovation and Improvement, I was involved with the creation of the Investing in Innovation Fund (i3), especially its initial design. One of the things that the Investing in Innovation Fund did is it set up a framework for awarding competitive grants based on the level of evidence that a particular project or innovation had. That framework, where you get a little bit of money if you have a little evidence and a lot of money if you have a lot of evidence, is pretty fundamental to establishing not only a framework for evidence but also an innovation pipeline, and setting the tone for the education sector to have the incentives to create solutions that actually improve outcomes and have rigor to back up their results.

So that initial program, i3, set the context for being able to do that same kind of tiered-evidence work across multiple programs, and in fact it's embedded in the regulations at the Department of Education and can be applied to any competitive program at this point. It also created the context for us to work with the National Science Foundation on creating common evidence standards that are shared between the Department of Education and NSF and look like they may be adopted by other agencies as well.

WHY DID YOU EMBRACE A MONEYBALL APPROACH, AND WHAT WERE YOUR BIGGEST CONCERNS BEFORE YOU GOT STARTED?

What you call the Moneyball approach to us was a simple belief in the power of data and evidence to drive improved decision making and outcomes. From the beginning of our work, we've recognized the need for new and bold solutions as well as the need to do a much better job taking what works to scale.

What that means is three things: The first is to get breakthrough solutions, we need to challenge people to achieve specific outcomes and then let them have a fair amount of freedom about how they do that. The big question in this approach is "Do you have a mechanism to recognize and select those breakthroughs and the rigor to tell whether they really worked?" The second is that we need to spend the majority of our dollars on things that have a high probability of success. Probability of success is highly correlated, obviously, with having evidence that something works. The problem with that is, at the beginning in education and many other sectors, you're not going to have a lot of interventions with real evidence. Thus the third and final implication is that what we want to do is not only encourage folks to have evidence but also to build evidence of what works. What you're going to have is data for measuring performance, data for measuring continuous improvement, and over time, you're able to take that data and turn it into evidence. All of that is important to ultimately building a large portfolio of things that work and perhaps most importantly, a culture of using data and evidence to improve practice and outcomes. That's all great, but the time it takes to build each of these critical elements undermines the momentum we need to get broad adoption by policy makers and practitioners.

WHAT WAS YOUR TOUGHEST OBSTACLE IN GETTING YOUR ORGANIZATION TO EMBRACE THIS APPROACH?

I think the biggest barrier to getting organizations to adopt this approach is fear.

Fear that because the education space is not evidence rich, meaning there aren't a lot of things out there with rigorous evidence, there would be a limited field of potential applicants. We overcame much of this after receiving thousands of applications in the first competition, but we also had to get comfortable with the lag time for more applicants to have the evidence required to meet the highest evidence requirements.

Fear that this approach requires a level of expertise about evaluation and other domains that we don't have in our traditional competitions or the program teams that support them. And so we had to partner with the Institute of Education Sciences (IES) to find expert reviewers as well as work with them over the years to train new reviewers. In this way, we increased the capacity not only to review these kinds of applications but also to help applicants be really clear about what the evidence standards are and how they meet them with the design of their studies.

Fear that this was more work in a time of declining resources. As I mentioned, running these kinds of competitions takes time and coordination. We had to be able to validate the studies that were submitted and, with very limited time windows to receive applications, select winners and make awards. And so anything that cut into that limited time was seen as somewhat of a burden. Getting folks comfortable with the need to do a lot of work in a short period of time and recognize that the value-add was worth that effort was also extremely important. Once we did it and people saw the benefits, including the substance of their work, the team embraced it pretty wholeheartedly, and that's why you're seeing the tiered-evidence structure moving across the Department of Education pretty quickly.

WHAT ARE YOUR TOP THREE KEY INSIGHTS OR LESSONS LEARNED?

The first insight is that using evidence to set and prioritize eligibility, selection, and funding level is essential to making evidence-based programming work. Perhaps more important than that for the long term is providing the resources and support for applicants and ultimately grantees to build new evidence for the field.

The second insight is that we should have little expectation that applicants or their advisers, even those who have been trained in general research methodologies, will know how to design rigorous studies without assistance. What we found is that without technical assistance the initial evaluation designs of our first cohort of almost 50 grantees would have led to a maximum of 25 of them winding up with studies that met our standards for rigor. What we were able to do by providing technical assistance is to get that number up to 42 of them that have designed rigorous studies that we're now going to have as part of the portfolio of evidence about what does and what doesn't work.

The third key insight is that you need to create a continuum of evidence—from the very early stage, where you have basically just a promising idea and a really good logic model, all the way up to gold-standard evidence supported by randomized controlled trials. The continuum needs to be very clear, and designed to encourage both new and early-stage ideas and rigor at every stage of development. People often think that just because they're doing something new that rigorous analysis of the process and the outcomes should be reserved for later-stage development when you have a large-scale study that can be completed. But in fact, at every stage of development, with data collection, analysis, and comparison, you can add appropriate rigor to determine whether things seem like they're on the right track and use that information to make adjustments improving design and implementation.

WHAT ADVICE DO YOU HAVE FOR OTHERS?

The advice I have for others is to jump in and get started. The tiered-evidence model is just one model of creating and using evidence and data to make thoughtful decisions about how to invest and allocate resources. There are many others. Where there's a strong evidence base, like we saw in the work around teen pregnancy, you can allow adoption of programs from a list of those that have rigorous evidence. Additionally, there are lots of ways to enter the work of using data and evidence to drive decisions when the evidence base is weak. The best thing to do is to get started and then to surround yourself with people who know what they're doing.

Appendix 2.

EXAMPLES OF MONEYBALL AT WORK

Stage 1 Supporting Development In The Earliest Years

2 Entering School Ready to Learn

3 Developing Grade-Level Reading, Math, and Other Critical Skills in Elementary School

4 Graduating from High School Ready for College and Career

5 Entering and then Completing Postsecondary Education or Training

6 Entering the Workforce

7 Giving a Second Chance to Young Adults Who Did Not Meet These Milestones

Want to see Moneyball in action? The following pages profile more than twenty of America's most-innovative and highest-impact social programs and initiatives from around the country.

These profiles demonstrate how organizations are using different types of evidence on the spectrum of rigor, and the choices they have made based on the organization's life cycle and the questions that are most valuable to answer.

They may take different approaches, but each profiled organization is committed to leveraging data, evaluation, and evidence of impact to make decisions and ultimately achieve its mission. Each organization is also committed to continuous learning, and many have already invested in rigorous evaluations of their work.

There are currently several efforts under way to understand which factors determine success throughout the stages of life. One such effort, the Social Genome Project, aims to build a data-rich model to allow policy makers to understand both the most fruitful pathways to success and the best strategies to get there.

In recent years, the Obama administration has taken a related approach, with initiatives like My Brother's Keeper, with the goal of targeting policies to these key moments in children's lives.

Because this has become an increasingly common way for policy makers to consider social interventions, the profiles included here are categorized in a roughly similar way. These are the essential moments on the path toward middle class success:

1. Supporting development in the earliest years;

2. Entering school ready to learn;

3. Developing grade-level reading, math, and other critical skills in elementary school;

4. Graduating from high school ready for college and career;

5. Entering and then completing postsecondary education or training;

6. Entering the workforce; and

7. Giving a second chance to young adults who did not meet these milestones.

The following profiles, based on publicly available information, internal analysis, and organization interviews, illustrate that the type of change described throughout this book is indeed possible and already making a difference in the lives of young people, their families, and their communities today. We hope this book will help encourage others to follow and to both replicate and scale similar efforts, as well as inspire action at all levels of government that will help ensure the growth and sustainability of such efforts over time. These profiles are cursory by design, but we hope they will pique your curiosity and encourage you to learn more about the extraordinary progress we see today.

Stage 1.

SUPPORTING DEVELOPMENT IN THE EARLIEST YEARS

NURSE-FAMILY PARTNERSHIP

Nurse-Family Partnership is a nurse home-visiting program focusing on low-income, first-time families. NFP sends specially trained nurses to visit with expectant mothers over the course of their pregnancy and for two years after the birth of their child. NFP nurses teach parenting and life skills, provide health and nutrition advice, and help mothers gain access to vocational and educational programs.

EVIDENCE

Three decades of rigorous research and randomized controlled trials have validated the effectiveness of Nurse-Family Partnership. NFP also has a research agenda to rigorously test program modifications that it is considering adopting. To understand the effectiveness of the program when scaled nationally, NFP is participating in MIHOPE and MIHOPE-Strong Start, two randomized multisite national evaluations of home visiting being conducted by outside evaluators (MDRC and research partners) and funded by the Department of Health and Human Services. Long-term follow-up studies have shown that contrary to mothers and children in the control group, NFP mothers are more economically self-sufficient and more likely to avoid criminal behavior, and NFP children are healthier and more productive. According to the RAND Corporation, every dollar invested in the program returns up to $5.70—a net return of more than $20,000 per family served.

PERFORMANCE

NFP participation consistently results in enhanced prenatal care, improved child health and development, and strengthened economic self-sufficiency for families. By 2013, 26,350 mothers across forty-three states were enrolled in NFP, more than double the enrollment from the program's inception in 2003. In 2013, 74 percent of the mothers enrolled in the program did not become pregnant after the birth of their first child—up from 68 percent in 2007.

PLANS FOR GROWTH

Through 2014, NFP expects to have enrolled upward of thirty thousand mothers and to have increased the number of nurse home visitors from 1,470 to 2,168. By focusing growth on states with an existing NFP presence, as well as states that are receiving federal Maternal, Infant, and Early Childhood Home Visiting (MIECHV) program funding, NFP intends to reach an annual enrollment of sixty thousand mothers by the end of 2018.

FOR MORE INFORMATION, VISIT WWW.NURSEFAMILYPARTNERSHIP.ORG.

ENTERING SCHOOL READY TO LEARN

APPLETREE

AppleTree closes the achievement gap by providing underserved three- and four-year-olds with the cognitive and social-emotional skills they need to thrive in kindergarten. AppleTree is comprised of AppleTree Institute for Education Innovation, a research and development arm, and AppleTree Early Learning, a multisite charter preschool. AppleTree employs a research-to-practice model to ensure continuous improvement of Every Child Ready, their comprehensive preschool instructional model that features content, professional development, and aligned progress-monitoring tools and assessments. Ten other preschools and community-based organizations in the nation's capital have adopted Every Child Ready.

EVIDENCE

AppleTree continuously monitors student and teacher performance in order to ensure quality teacher-child interactions and strong child outcomes. Every Child Ready is based on a robust evidentiary data set that utilizes early-childhood education research from leading academic and philanthropic institutions. In 2010, the U.S. Department of Education validated the Every Child Ready program, and AppleTree as a whole, by awarding it the highly competitive Investing in Innovation (i3) grant to further develop the program.

PERFORMANCE

AppleTree's programs reach more than 1,400 young students each year. Every Child Ready is a comprehensive instructional model that includes "how to teach, what to teach, and how to know it's being done." This approach improves teacher effectiveness and children's learning. More than 90 percent of AppleTree students score in the normal range or above in standardized vocabulary and print-knowledge exams in 2012.

PLANS FOR GROWTH

AppleTree plans to educate more children while deploying the Every Child Ready curriculum into more partner classrooms. As AppleTree expands, it will rely on its strong foundation of evidence and data in order to produce consistently positive outcomes for its students.

FOR MORE INFORMATION, VISIT WWW.APPLETREEINSTITUTE.ORG.

TULSA EDUCARE

Tulsa Educare—part of the national Educare network—uses very early childhood education to enhance underprivileged children's school readiness. Tulsa Educare focuses on building early, positive experience in a safe environment so as to foster cognitive and language development. Educare serves upward of five hundred children from birth through four years old at three locations in Tulsa, Oklahoma. The schools are specially designed to nurture early learning and to narrow the achievement gap.

EVIDENCE

The University of Oklahoma Early Childhood Education Institute collects data on Tulsa Educare to assess language and literacy skills and social and emotional development and to document student progress. On a national level, Tulsa Educare is part of a study at the University of North Carolina that uses local data to evaluate all Educare programs. This research has determined that Educare programs are more effective the earlier a child enrolls in the program and that positive results persist upon the student entering kindergarten.

PERFORMANCE

English-speaking students who entered the Tulsa Educare system at two years scored 5.6 points higher on vocabulary tests than students who entered at four years. The positive effects are heightened for dual-language learners. DLLs that entered Tulsa Educare at age two scored 16.4 points higher than their peers that entered at age four. The Tulsa results generally sync with national Educare results, which show that the earlier students enter the program, the higher levels of academic achievement and school readiness they demonstrate.

PLANS FOR GROWTH

Tulsa Educare continues to grow and evolve by using feedback from parents and evaluators to expand their existing programs.

FOR MORE INFORMATION, VISIT WWW.TULSAEDUCARE.ORG.

DEVELOPING GRADE-LEVEL READING, MATH, AND OTHER CRITICAL SKILLS IN ELEMENTARY SCHOOL

BUILDING EDUCATED LEADERS FOR LIFE

Building Educated Leaders for Life (BELL) provides comprehensive academic support to students most at risk of failing grades K–8. BELL's programs feature small-group instruction, enrichment courses, community service, personal mentorship, and initiatives to encourage parental engagement. BELL's curriculum adheres to state and national standards and is delivered in partnership with local schools and districts during instructional and after-school hours, as well as over the summer.

EVIDENCE

A randomized controlled trial completed by the Urban Institute showed that BELL's summer program has a statistically significant impact on reading achievement for elementary school students, equivalent to about one month's worth of learning. The report went on to say, "Few out-of-school-time programs have produced evidence of effectiveness when evaluated in such a rigorous manner." A study of BELL's middle school model is currently under way.

PERFORMANCE

Starting in 2007, BELL enrolled 7,309 students in its programs. By 2013, it enrolled 12,828 students. After completing BELL's school-year program, students who enrolled in 2013 gained more than three months' worth of instruction in reading and math.

PLANS FOR GROWTH

With BELL's recent expansion, its programs are currently delivered in Massachusetts, New York, New Jersey, Maryland, North Carolina, Ohio, and California. Additional reach to eight other communities has been achieved through an innovation partnership with a nationally networked organization. BELL plans to enhance the long-term prospects of its summer programs by strengthening its business-development office, regional advisory councils, and base of district and philanthropic support. By 2017 BELL projects to enroll nearly twenty thousand students.

FOR MORE INFORMATION, VISIT WWW.EXPERIENCEBELL.ORG.

KNOWLEDGE IS POWER PROGRAM (KIPP)

There are currently 162 KIPP public charter schools operating in twenty states and the District of Columbia. KIPP public charter schools are serving fifty-eight thousand students in more than thirty rural and urban communities. More than 88 percent of KIPP's students are from low-income families and eligible for the federal free or reduced-price meals program, and 95 percent are African American or Latino. KIPP's mission is to create a respected, influential, and national network of public schools that are successful in helping students from educationally underserved communities develop the knowledge, skills, character, and habits needed to succeed in college and the competitive world beyond.

EVIDENCE

KIPP has a long-standing commitment to independent research on its effectiveness. In 2008, Mathematica Policy Research began a multi-year longitudinal study of KIPP middle schools. Mathematica has released two reports from the study, in 2010 and 2013. The 2013 report highlighted that (1) KIPP middle schools made significant gains in reading, math, science, and social studies across all grades, and (2) the magnitude of KIPP's achievement impacts is substantial. Students showed gains equivalent to an extra 8 months of learning in reading, 11 months in math, 14 months in science, and 11 months in social studies. Mathematica's research also included a test of higher-thinking skills, which students could not have prepared for in advance. On this exam, KIPP students showed substantial gains in all tested subjects and across all grades—demonstrating that KIPP's gains could not be explained by teaching to the test.

PERFORMANCE

Nationally, 55 percent of KIPP students outperform their fellow eighth graders in reading and 59 percent outperform their peers in math. To date, 93 percent of KIPP middle school students have gone on to complete their high school education, 82 percent of KIPP alumni have attended college, and 44 percent have earned a bachelor's degree. KIPP's alumni are exceeding the national average of college completion, higher than the average American's and more than four times the rate for low-income students.

PLANS FOR GROWTH

KIPP aspires to open twenty or more new schools each year. By 2020, KIPP pledges to double the number of students they serve.

FOR MORE INFORMATION, VISIT WWW.KIPP.ORG.

READING PARTNERS

Reading Partners provides individualized, one-on-one tutoring for elementary school students who are six months to more than two years behind grade level in reading proficiency. The national non-profit operates reading centers in underserved schools in urban communities, harnessing the power of community volunteers to deliver a proven, evidence-based curriculum in biweekly tutoring sessions.

EVIDENCE

From 2012 to 2013, MDRC conducted a rigorous study of nineteen Reading Partners schools across three states involving more than 1,200 youth. Early results suggest that Reading Partners has a positive impact on all aspects of reading proficiency—comprehension, fluency, and sight-word reading. The final MDRC report is expected in 2015.

PERFORMANCE

Eighty-nine percent of Reading Partners participants accelerate their rate of learning. On average, students gain 1.6 months of reading skills for every month spent in the program. In 2011, Reading Partners served 1,900 youth. By 2013, it had served 4,814 youth. Reading Partners has been shown to have positive impacts on a wide variety of students, irrespective of grade, gender, or language.

PLANS FOR GROWTH

Reading Partners recently expanded its operations to Maryland, New York, California, and Washington, DC. By partnering with like-minded philanthropic organizations, Reading Partners has also established new sites in Colorado. Reading Partners will support this group by strengthening its regional and national offices, which will provide a foundation for planned expansions to Boston and Seattle.

FOR MORE INFORMATION, VISIT WWW.READINGPARTNERS.ORG.

STRIVETOGETHER CRADLE TO CAREER NETWORK

The StriveTogether Cradle to Career Network is comprised of forty-nine local community partnerships around the United States that have come together to erase the educational-achievement gap in underserved communities. StriveTogether relies on evidence-based solutions and a culture of constant improvement to assist communities in building the partnerships needed to improve indicators in six outcome areas: kindergarten readiness, early-grade reading, middle-grade math, high school graduation, college entrance, and degree completion. The initial flagship community was in Cincinnati and northern Kentucky, where they launched the Strive Partnership in 2006. Three hundred cross-sector leaders came together to agree on a set of common goals and success indicators for their community and committed to use data to identify and build on what worked already, filling in gaps with evidence-based practice only as needed. Since then, the national StriveTogether Cradle to Career Network has expanded to twenty-six states and the District of Columbia, with local partnerships each using a common methodology known as the Theory of Action to contextualize the work for the unique needs of their community.

EVIDENCE

It is difficult to use RCTs and other rigorous evaluation tools to assess the impact of a community-wide intervention like StriveTogether. But FSG, the Bridgespan Group, and the Carnegie Foundation for the Advancement of Teaching have all released independent reports that have looked at the components of the StriveTogether model and see enormous promise. StriveTogether provides a useful example for how communities can set goals for improving student outcomes, gather and use data to measure progress toward these goals, and align public and philanthropic dollars toward what is working.

PERFORMANCE

The Strive Partnership, StriveTogether's flagship program in Cincinnati and northern Kentucky, has proven enormously effective in improving students' educational achievement. Over the first five years of the program, kindergarten readiness grew by eleven points to 55 percent. Fourth-grade reading-achievement scores increased 16 percent. Additionally, Strive Partnership was responsible for an 11 percent increase in college graduation and a 10 percent increase in college enrollment.

PLANS FOR GROWTH

StriveTogether is working with Cradle to Career Network members to actively learn from their experiences—"failing forward" to identify emerging standards of practice for the collective impact movement. Communities are provided with a set of tools to help meet the initial progress milestones outlined in the Theory of Action and must demonstrate they have made significant progress before becoming an official member. This group of highly committed network members are then formulating tools and resources for the field that are available on an open-source platform and through strategic assistance that can help expedite progress. The collective goal of the network is to establish fifteen "Proof Point Communities"—defined as meeting the systems-change progress milestones in the Theory of Action and seeing sustained improvements in a majority of student outcome indicators—by 2018.

FOR MORE INFORMATION, VISIT WWW.STRIVETOGETHER.ORG.

SUCCESS FOR ALL

Success for All is a comprehensive, research-backed strategy aimed at improving underperforming schools. Success for All coaches teachers, integrates parents and the community with the school, engages students in rich discussion, and overhauls the curriculum with a primary emphasis on reading. Success for All also places a priority on continuous, rigorous research and evaluation—of students, teachers, programs, and the entire foundation itself.

EVIDENCE

In a three-year randomized controlled trial, Success for All students performed at significantly higher levels than the control group. In those three years, the achievement gap between black and white students was cut in half.

A meta-analysis in the *Review of Educational Research* found that out of twenty-nine similar programs, only three, including Success for All, demonstrated the "strongest evidence of effectiveness." Research from past Success for All implementations has shown that cost savings from grade repetition and from limiting the practice of sending students with learning disabilities to special-education programs cover all Success for All expenses within five years.

PERFORMANCE

More than a thousand schools, totaling two million students from the United States, the United Kingdom, and Canada have adopted Success for All. Fifth graders in Success for All schools perform, on average, at a full grade level higher than fifth graders in comparable schools. In 2010, Success for All was the highest-rated scale-up program in the U.S. Department of Education's i3 competition.

PLANS FOR GROWTH

Success for All will continue to grow by bringing its high-impact program to new schools. As data tools, funding scenarios, and mandated curricula change, Success for All will constantly adapt to ensure that it is on the front line of school reform.

FOR MORE INFORMATION, VISIT WWW.SUCCESSFORALL.ORG.

TEACH FOR AMERICA

Teach for America (TFA) recruits and develops a diverse corps of outstanding individuals of all academic disciplines to commit to teach for two years in high-need schools and become lifelong leaders in the movement to end educational inequity. Today, 10,500 corps members in fifty urban and rural regions across the country serve 660,000 students, while nearly 37,000 alumni work from across sectors to ensure that all children have access to an excellent education.

EVIDENCE

A growing body of rigorous independent research demonstrates that Teach for America teachers are having a positive impact in the classroom. Studies by Edvance Research Inc., Mathematica Policy Research, and Harvard University have found that corps members and alumni tend to be more effective in promoting students' academic achievement than other teachers of math and science in the same schools, and at least as effective in other tested subjects. In North Carolina, TFA teachers were found to be the most effective in student gains compared to other new teachers. Additionally, TFA teachers in Memphis and Nashville are among the most effective math, science, and social science teachers for fourth through eighth graders in Tennessee. In the 2013 National Principal Survey, 84 percent of TFA's partner principals said they would hire a TFA member again if given the opportunity.

PERFORMANCE

Since 1990, TFA has reached more than three million children nationwide. For students grades 3–9, TFA teachers were shown to have a substantially positive impact in academic growth for reading and math.

Secondary-school students taught by TFA teachers generally receive the equivalent of 2.6 extra months of math education when compared to students taught by teachers from other teacher-preparation programs.

PLANS FOR GROWTH

TFA tailors growth according to the needs of regional and community partners, placing a particular emphasis on recruiting and developing individuals who share the racial and economic backgrounds of the students the organization serves. From career teachers to school leaders to policy and advocacy agents, the organization aims to foster and accelerate alumni leadership that will drive lasting, systemic change for students and communities.

FOR MORE INFORMATION, VISIT WWW.TEACHFORAMERICA.ORG.

Stage 4.

GRADUATING FROM HIGH SCHOOL READY FOR COLLEGE AND CAREER

CITIZEN SCHOOLS

Citizen Schools aims to improve the level of educational achievement of underserved students aged 11–14 by working with middle schools around the country to expand the learning day.

Citizen Schools' expanded day programs help students raise academic performance, as well as prepare them for high school and college, by engaging AmeriCorps members to lead supported, standards-aligned practice in English language arts and math and target the development of twenty-first-century skills. In addition, volunteer "Citizen Teachers" expose students to postsecondary and career options and engage them in long-term projects that culminate in a presentation to family and community members.

EVIDENCE

A 2010 matched-comparison longitudinal study completed by Policy Studies Associates found multiple statistically significant indicators of Citizen Schools' efficacy in improving the academic outcomes of participating students.

At the moment, Citizen Schools is working with Abt Associates to conduct a multi-year, quasi-experimental evaluation of its Expanded Learning Time (ELT) model and is also launching a randomized study of its apprenticeships in the STEM fields.

Results from those studies are not yet available, but the most recent analysis found that schools that implemented the ELT model gained over ten percentage points in proficiency over a two-year period, which exceeds the U.S. Department of Education's standard for school turnaround.

PERFORMANCE

In 2000, Citizen Schools served 401 youth. By 2013, program participation was over ten times higher—with 4,832 youth served.

In 2010, 59 percent of Citizen School middle schoolers went on to attend "college track" high schools—more than twice the standard rate. Seventy-one percent of Citizen Schools students graduated high school on time, a rate twelve points higher than that of nonparticipating students.

PLANS FOR GROWTH

Based on a strategic plan finalized in 2014, Citizen Schools hopes to build deep partnerships with eight to ten school districts and increase total student enrollment to eight thousand by 2016–2017.

FOR MORE INFORMATION, VISIT WWW.CITIZENSCHOOLS.ORG.

CITY YEAR

City Year aims to bridge the gap in high-poverty communities between the educational, social, and emotional support students need and what area schools are capable of providing. Diverse teams of City Year AmeriCorps members work with students—from elementary through high school—building their academic skills, increasing their attendance, developing their self-confidence, and engaging with their families. By helping students build their skills and confidence, City Year guides students on a path toward a sustainable and successful academic career.

EVIDENCE

City Year programs are driven by both proprietary research and publicly available studies from experts in the education field. Local programs are rigorously evaluated to ensure they are efficiently meeting their goals and providing the necessary support to disadvantaged students. City Year, along with partners from Johns Hopkins University and Communities in Schools, is engaged in one of the nation's largest randomized controlled research studies of secondary-school improvement, led by MDRC and supported in part through the U.S. Department of Education's Investing in Innovation Fund.

PERFORMANCE

During the 2012–2013 school year, City Year students spent 14,600 more hours in school than in the year before. Fifty-four percent of students in grades 6–9 went from failing to passing their ELA course. When given a literary assessment, 82 percent of City Year 3–5 graders and 65 percent of 6–9 graders improved their scores.

City Year closely tracks its perception from teachers and school leaders by assessing areas such as its ability to support teachers in the classroom, improve their differentiated instruction practices, and improve overall school climate. For example, 77 percent of teachers report that corps members helped differentiate instruction, 91 percent of teachers report that corps members helped foster a positive environment for learning in the classroom, and 80 percent of principals or liaisons report that corps members establish a college- and career-going culture.

PLANS FOR GROWTH

By 2023, City Year plans to serve more than seven hundred thousand students every day in more than a thousand schools in thirty-eight cities that account for two-thirds of the nation's urban dropouts. City Year plans to support this expansion by continuing to strengthen its academic and socioemotional interventions, growing in new and existing markets, building a pipeline of engaged alumni, and securing larger, longer-term capital investments.

FOR MORE INFORMATION, VISIT WWW.CITYYEAR.ORG.

COMMUNITIES IN SCHOOLS

Communities in Schools (CIS) is the nation's largest and most effective dropout-prevention organization and the only one proven to both decrease dropout rates and increase graduation rates. CIS works hand in hand with schools, communities, and families to surround students with a caring network of support to help them stay in school and succeed in life. CIS has nearly 42,000 volunteers on the ground, working in more than 2,200 K–12 public schools in the most challenged communities in twenty-six states and the District of Columbia, serving 1.3 million young people and their families every year.

By providing students with a one-on-one relationship with a caring adult, CIS creates a safe place to learn and grow, a healthy start to a healthy future, a path toward marketable skills upon graduation, and a chance to give back to peers and the community.

EVIDENCE

In 2012, consultants and economic modelers at Economic Modeling Specialists International calculated that, on average, every dollar invested in CIS creates $11.60 worth of economic benefits for the community. In 2010, ICF International completed a multiyear study of CIS, which included a quasi-experimental school-level study and student-level randomized controlled trials. ICF found that, when implemented with fidelity, schools with the CIS model of integrated student supports experienced lower dropout rates and greater on-time graduation rates than similar schools without CIS.

Additionally, the randomized controlled trials demonstrated that providing case-managed services to high-need students during the transition years (sixth and ninth grade) resulted in fewer drop-outs, fewer students retained in grade, higher credit completion, better overall grade point average, and better attendance.

CIS is currently undertaking additional research to build the evidence base used by many organizations to provide support for integrated student-support programs. For example, under the Social Innovation Fund grant program, MDRC is currently evaluating the impact of the full CIS comprehensive model by using a comparative interrupted-time-series design, and is evaluating the implementation and impact of the student case-management component of the full model by using a randomized controlled trial. Results from these studies are expected in 2015.

PERFORMANCE

During the 2012–2013 school year, CIS provided nearly 1.3 million students across 2,250 sites with whole-school interventions, and an additional 134,000 students received intensive, case-managed services. Ninety-two percent of these students qualified for free or reduced-price lunch, and more than 80 percent were minorities. The individual accomplishments for these students were overwhelmingly positive. For students with specific goals:

- 75 percent met attendance goals
- 86 percent met school behavior improvement goals
- 84 percent met academic improvement goals

Additionally, 97 percent of nonseniors were promoted to the next grade, and 96 percent of seniors graduated.

PLANS FOR GROWTH

When the 2013–2014 data are in, CIS is expected to have realized a 10 percent growth in students served over the past three years. By the 2014–2015 school year, CIS plans to expand its presence in 137 new schools across twenty-eight communities to reach approximately 80,000 additional students. CIS is projected to serve 1.4 million students in the 2014–2015 school year.

FOR MORE INFORMATION, VISIT WWW.COMMUNITIESINSCHOOLS.ORG.

DIPLOMAS NOW

Diplomas Now works in America's largest cities to identify middle and high school students who are most at risk of dropping out and to provide the targeted and intensive resources needed to put them on the path to graduation. Diplomas Now combines whole-school reform supports provided by Johns Hopkins University's Talent Development Secondary model, with individualized student supports provided by City Year and Communities in Schools.

Diplomas Now works to identify the key factors that lead to dropouts: poor attendance, bad behavior, and failure in English or math courses. Diplomas Now helps each school develop an early-warning-indicator system, and Diplomas Now utilizes this data system to inform both whole-school reform initiatives and individualized student supports. The organization deploys a team of caring adults at each school to provide social, emotional, and academic supports for students, to help schools restructure to increase their positive impact on students, and to offer both extra-help curricula for students and professional development for teachers.

EVIDENCE

Diplomas Now started as a pilot with one 700-student middle school in Philadelphia in 2008–2009. Today, it serves 27,000 students in thirteen cities. Diplomas Now's methodology is based on research by Johns Hopkins University that shows that half of all dropouts can be identified by the end of sixth grade. Course failure, lax attendance, and poor behavior are the key indicators. In 2014, supported

by a federal i3 validation grant, Diplomas Now is currently participating in the largest ever randomized field trial of secondary-school
reform models, including more than sixty secondary schools and
thirty thousand students. MDRC and ICF International released an
implementation report from this evaluation in 2014, and additional
reports about the impact of the Diplomas Now model are expected
in 2015.

PERFORMANCE

During the 2012–2013 school year, Diplomas Now achieved a 41
percent reduction in students with poor attendance, a 70 percent
reduction in suspensions, a 69 percent reduction in English-class
failure, and a 52 percent reduction in math-class failures of the
students that started the year without problems in attendance,
behavior, or academic performance—90 percent stayed on track for
the entire year.

PLANS FOR GROWTH

Diplomas Now has undertaken a large fund-raising campaign to
sustain the ongoing, multi-year independent i3 evaluation that will
provide crucial evidence regarding the efficacy of their programs.
The results of the study could potentially lead to significant public
and private investment in Diplomas Now to increase the numbers
of schools Diplomas Now serves in its existing cities and to expand
to new sites.

FOR MORE INFORMATION, VISIT WWW.DIPLOMASNOW.ORG.

GATEWAY TO COLLEGE NATIONAL NETWORK

Gateway to College National Network (GtCNN) is an alternative education network that aims to create educational opportunities for young people who have dropped out of high school or who are considering dropping out. The program allows youths to simultaneously earn a high school diploma and college credits. GtCNN provides students with resource specialists to advise and mentor them over the course of their studies. In addition, GtCNN provides local sites assistance in training, planning, development, and technology.

EVIDENCE

In addition to studying internal data collected by GtCNN, the network is working with MDRC on an implementation study and an internal small-scale random assignment study to assess the feasibility of conducting a larger randomized controlled trial. The study aims to assess the implementation and outcomes of GtCNN and will be completed by 2015.

PERFORMANCE

In 2011, GtCNN served 3,391 youth, 44 percent of whom stayed in the program between academic years. By 2013, GtCNN served 4,228 youth, 51 percent of whom stayed in the program between academic years. GtCNN participants had an average high school attendance rate of 81 percent, despite the fact that they were enrolled at schools with traditionally poor attendance. Students who graduate from GtCNN earn, on average, thirty-six college semester credits.

PLANS FOR GROWTH

By 2015, GtCNN will establish nineteen new sites around the country. This growth will allow GtCNN to double its number of youth served.

As the national GtCNN organization grows, it will focus on supporting its regional offices, spearheading new local fund-raising efforts, and advocating for initiatives that promote, further, and support high school graduation and college preparedness at the state and national levels.

FOR MORE INFORMATION, VISIT WWW.GATEWAYTOCOLLEGE.ORG.

SMALL SCHOOLS OF CHOICE

New York City has the largest public school system in the United States. In 2002, the city began to close large underperforming high schools, while creating hundreds of what MDRC researchers call Small Schools of Choice (SSCs) open to students of all levels of achievement. In 2002, the city instituted a district-wide high school admissions process that emphasized student choice, and began establishing over a hundred new academically nonselective small public schools that were open to students with widely varying academic backgrounds. Incoming ninth-grade students now have over four hundred high school options available to them. They are assigned a slot based on a lottery-preference system. MDRC used this system to develop a study of SSCs, ultimately finding that they led to substantially increased graduation rates.

EVIDENCE

The most recent MDRC findings about SSCs are based on data that tracked more than 12,000 students from 192 lotteries for 84 SSCs. This sample represents three annual cohorts of first-time ninth graders who entered high school in the fall of 2005, 2006, or 2007. The study does not compare SSC students to their counterparts in chronically struggling large schools but rather to their counterparts in all other public high schools operated in the city.

PERFORMANCE

MDRC found that, on average, enrolling in these new Small Schools—most of which serve students from underprivileged minority communities—increased four-year graduation rates by 9.5 percentage points (to 70.4 percent for students enrolled in SSCs from 60.9 for their control group counterparts). Nearly every sub-group of students—including male and female minority students, academically struggling students, and low-income students—saw marked improvements. Principals and teachers at the twenty-five schools with the best and strongest evidence for improvement report that academic rigor and personal relationships with students contribute to the effectiveness of their schools.

A new report, to be released by MDRC in the fall of 2014, contains early evidence that suggests that the effects of SSCs on students' high school graduation rates will be sustained through future effects on enrollment and persistence in postsecondary education.

In 2013, researchers from MIT and Duke released a study that replicated and confirmed MDRC's findings. These researchers found results that indicated positive effects on students in SSCs. In addition, the MIT-Duke study found that the positive effects on students are sustained when SSC students go on to college.

PLANS FOR GROWTH

With encouraging evidence from third-party evaluators, the New York City Department of Education is expected to continue opening Small Schools of Choice.

FOR MORE INFORMATION, VISIT WWW.MDRC.ORG/PROJECT/NEW-YORK-CITY-SMALL-SCHOOLS-CHOICE-EVALUATION.

ENTERING AND THEN COMPLETING POSTSECONDARY EDUCATION OR TRAINING

CITY UNIVERSITY OF NEW YORK (CUNY) ACCELERATED STUDY IN ASSOCIATE PROGRAMS (ASAP)

CUNY ASAP, launched in 2007 with funding from the New York City Center for Economic Opportunity, is designed to help more community-college students graduate and help them graduate more quickly. The program is designed to simultaneously address multiple potential barriers to student success and to address them for up to three years. ASAP requires students to attend college full-time and encourages them to take developmental courses early. The program provides enhanced career services, enhanced tutoring, and comprehensive guidance from an adviser with a small caseload. ASAP offers blocked or linked courses for the first year and offers an ASAP seminar for a few semesters, covering topics such as goal setting and study skills. The program provides free textbooks and a tuition waiver that covers any gap between financial aid and college tuition and fees. It also provides free MetroCards for use on public transportation, contingent on participation in key program services.

EVIDENCE

MDRC conducted an evaluation of ASAP at three CUNY community colleges, which targeted low-income students who needed one or two developmental (or remedial) courses. The randomized controlled trial found that ASAP dramatically improved student academic outcomes over three years. ASAP increased enrollment in college and credit accumulation. Importantly, the program almost doubled graduation rates at the three-year point and increased the proportion of students who transferred to a four-year school. The effects found in the RCT—the largest MDRC has found for a community-college reform—along with the results from CUNY's internal study of ASAP, indicate that ASAP's package of supports and requirements has been unusually successful in improving outcomes for low income students.

PERFORMANCE

In MDRC's evaluation of ASAP, at the three-year point, the cost per degree in ASAP was lower than for regular college services. Because ASAP generated so many more graduates than the usual college services, the cost per degree was lower despite the substantial investment required to operate ASAP.

PLANS FOR GROWTH

Based on ASAP's positive effects and on additional funding from the City of New York, CUNY is substantially expanding the program, with a goal of serving over thirteen thousand students by fall 2016 across the six community colleges that originally operated the program, and additional CUNY colleges. In addition, CUNY and MDRC are collaborating on replicating ASAP at three colleges in Ohio and possibly others.

FOR MORE INFORMATION ABOUT ASAP OR MDRC'S EVALUATION, VISIT WWW. CUNY.EDU/ACADEMICS/PROGRAMS/NOTABLE/ASAP.HTML AND WWW.MDRC.ORG/ PROJECT/EVALUATION-ACCELERATED-STUDY-ASSOCIATE-PROGRAMS-ASAP-DEVELOPMENTAL-EDUCATION-STUDENTS#FEATURED_CONTENT.

Stage 6.

ENTERING THE WORKFORCE

THE CENTER FOR EMPLOYMENT OPPORTUNITIES

The Center for Employment Opportunities (CEO) helps people who have recently been released from jail or prison find and keep steady jobs.

CEO offers a weeklong preemployment vocational class, followed by transitional employment on one of its work crews. From there, participants are generally placed in a full-time, unsubsidized, private-sector job within two to three months.

EVIDENCE

A three-year randomized controlled trial conducted by MDRC found that CEO reduced recidivism in participants by up to 22 percent. MDRC went on to note, "Reductions in recidivism are difficult to achieve and have rarely been seen in rigorous evaluations such as this one." Based on these findings, the evaluation and Vera Institute estimated the program's total net benefit to taxpayers was between $4,100 and $8,300 per participant.

PERFORMANCE

In 2004, CEO served 1,648 participants. By 2013, the program had more than doubled—serving 3,359 participants. Of that first class, 16 percent of participants were still employed or in school after twelve months. By 2013, 61 percent of participants either held a job or were in school one year out of the program.

PLANS FOR GROWTH

CEO plans to complement its existing programs in New York City and upstate New York with classes, work sites, and job placements in Oklahoma and California. By 2014, CEO expects the expansion to be complete—turning the Center for Employment Opportunities into a full-fledged national organization.

FOR MORE INFORMATION, VISIT WWW.CEOWORKS.ORG.

URBAN ALLIANCE

Urban Alliance has provided opportunities to disadvantaged youth to guide them toward gainful employment and economic self-sufficiency through paid internships, work-skills classes, and personal mentorship programs.

Urban Alliance's core initiative—the year-round High School Internship Program—offers young people an opportunity to not only acquire the necessary soft and technical skills to succeed professionally, but also practice them in a hands-on work environment. Interns receive their placement only after a rigorous four-week "pre-work" training period.

EVIDENCE

Urban Alliance is committed to its results and places a heavy emphasis on evaluation—both internal and external. Internally, Urban Alliance has created an assessment to gauge participant growth in professional skills, assessing progress four times per year and providing real-time feedback to participants. Urban Alliance also tracks and measures college enrollment and persistence through the National Student Clearinghouse—an organization that specializes in postsecondary enrollment verification. These data not only allow the organization to measure its own success, but they also provide insight on youth not persisting in school, providing Urban Alliance with a targeted follow-up roster.

In addition, Urban Alliance has partnered with the Urban Institute to complete a six-year randomized controlled trial study. While the final report will not be available until 2016, researchers have found signs of success through program observations and stakeholder interviews.

PERFORMANCE

Since its founding in 1996, Urban Alliance has placed more than 1,500 young people in professional internships. One hundred percent of program alumni graduate from high school. More than 75 percent enroll in college. And more than 80 percent of those who go to college reenroll for a second year.

PLANS FOR GROWTH

Since first serving youth over eighteen years ago in Washington, DC, Urban Alliance has continued to bridge the skills gap between young people and professional environments. After successful expansion to Baltimore, Chicago, and northern Virginia, with the assistance of the federally funded Social Innovation Fund (SIF), Urban Alliance is embarking on a strategic plan that will include further growth into new markets. Urban Alliance will continue to expand its footprint and bring new business partners into the fold with the goal of becoming the national voice for youth employment.

FOR MORE INFORMATION, VISIT WWW.THEURBANALLIANCE.ORG.

YEAR UP

Year Up is a one-year, rigorous job-training program for disconnected young adults between the ages of eighteen and twenty-four. Participants receive six months of professional and technical skills training followed by a six-month internship at a corporate partner. The program provides students with real-world experience and a growing professional network to help bridge the opportunity divide.

Year Up holds participants to high academic and professional standards but also offers high levels of support to empower its students to reach their potential and economic self-sufficiency. Throughout the one-year program, students earn college credits as well as weekly stipends.

EVIDENCE

Year Up is a participant in the federally funded Innovative Strategies for Increasing Self-Sufficiency (ISIS) study. The study is an evaluation of national strategies aimed at assisting low-income, low-skilled individuals.

PERFORMANCE

Since its launch in 2000, Year Up has served more than ten thousand young adults and has provided a pipeline of entry-level talent to more than 250 corporate partners.

One hundred percent of Year Up students who complete the first six months of the program are placed in internships. Four months after graduating from Year Up, 85 percent of alumni are either attending college full-time or are employed and earning an average of $30,000 per year. Over 90 percent of corporate partners would recommend the Year Up program to a colleague.

PLANS FOR GROWTH

Year Up's two-pronged growth strategy focuses on strengthening its relationships with corporate and community-college partners and shifting perceptions of urban youth—and what talent looks like—among employers across the United States.

FOR MORE INFORMATION, VISIT WWW.YEARUP.ORG.

YOUTHBUILD USA

YouthBuild USA supports a network of 264 YouthBuild programs sponsored by local community-based nonprofit or public entities. They are primarily funded directly through competitive grants from the U.S. Department of Labor under the DOL YouthBuild program authorized in the Workforce Innovations and Opportunity Act. In these programs low-income young adults aged 16–24 who have left high school without a diploma enroll full-time for 6–24 months. They spend half their time in hands-on job training building affordable housing for homeless and low-income people in their communities. They spend the other half in individualized YouthBuild classrooms completing their high school equivalency or diploma and preparing for college. Some YouthBuild programs also offer training in health care, technology, customer service, and other service-oriented career tracks. The program builds a safe and supportive peer group committed to the values inherent in community service and leadership. Students typically earn a stipend for their work building housing, and many earn AmeriCorps scholarships for postsecondary education.

EVIDENCE

An MIT study compared YouthBuild with other national youth job-training programs. It found that YouthBuild had the highest level of GED achievement. A Brandeis study of nine hundred YouthBuild graduates up to seven years after completion found 75 percent were in college or jobs averaging ten dollars an hour.

Researchers from Vanderbilt and NYU studied a targeted Youth-Build youthful-offender intervention program. The study found that every dollar spent on the program resulted in a social return of $7.80. Additionally, the researchers found that the program delivered between $134,000 and $536,000 worth of social benefits per participant.

MDRC is currently leading a random-assignment evaluation of YouthBuild. A total of seventy-five YouthBuild programs were selected to participate in the evaluation, and they enrolled nearly four thousand young adults into the study between August 2011 and January 2013. Findings will be published in 2017 and 2018. The evaluation is being funded by the U.S. Department of Labor, with additional support from the Corporation for National and Community Service.

PERFORMANCE

In 2013, 73 percent of enrollees in YouthBuild earned a GED, high school diploma, or an industry-recognized certificate. Fifty-five percent of all enrollees went on within three months of exit to postsecondary education, or jobs averaging $9.10 an hour. One year after entering YouthBuild, participants who had spent time in the criminal-justice system had a low, 10 percent recidivism rate. Since 1994, 130,000 YouthBuild participants have built over twenty-eight thousand units of affordable housing.

PLANS FOR GROWTH

YouthBuild USA is working to expand the resources available for local YouthBuild programs because thousands of young people seeking a second chance are turned away each year for lack of funds. YouthBuild USA is also advocating on the federal level for increased funds for all effective young-adult educational and employment programs.

FOR MORE INFORMATION, VISIT WWW.YOUTHBUILD.ORG.

GIVING A SECOND CHANCE TO YOUNG ADULTS WHO DID NOT MEET THESE MILESTONES

BECOMING A MAN

Becoming a Man (BAM), the signature initiative of Youth Guidance, is a Chicago-based program that offers in-school programs to underprivileged young men. BAM works with struggling and at-risk students to develop cognitive and conflict-resolution skills, as well as to reduce antisocial behavior, dropouts, and gang violence. BAM's social and emotional curriculum consists of small group sessions over the course of the year. Sessions focus on a particular skill and feature role-playing, group exercises, and a regular homework assignment that asks participants to practice the skill at home.

EVIDENCE

BAM is heavily based on research that shows that increased social and cognitive skills are highly predictive of future academic success and reduced involvement in gang or criminal activity. A randomized, controlled study conducted by the University of Chicago found that BAM greatly increased youths' academic engagement and performance, while decreasing participation in gangs and violent crime.

PERFORMANCE

In 2013, Becoming a Man reached 492 young men. The program will serve 2,000 young men in the 2014–2015 school year. Among participants, BAM has reduced arrests for nonviolent crimes by 36 percent and arrests for violent crimes by 44 percent.

The study also found that BAM resulted in social benefits of $49,000 to $119,000 per participant.

PLANS FOR GROWTH

BAM is expanding its reach, with hopes of reaching a total of forty-five Chicago-area schools by 2016. As the program expands, BAM will continue to implement a rigorous hiring and training process, while also enhancing its leadership team and revenue model.

FOR MORE INFORMATION, VISIT WWW.YOUTH-GUIDANCE.ORG.

FIRST PLACE FOR YOUTH

First Place for Youth helps at-risk youth who are currently in, and in the process of exiting from, the foster-care system. First Place works with young people to help them gain the skills they need, and the support they require, to lead successful lives. First Place provides access to housing, comprehensive case management, employment training, educational counseling, and financial-literacy classes to young people as a manner of smoothing the transition to a productive adulthood. First Place for Youth serves Los Angeles and the San Francisco Bay Area.

EVIDENCE

First Place for Youth has developed a robust performance-management system to track outcomes of youth in the program. At the end of 2013, First Place for Youth found the following:

- 86 percent of youth were employed
- 80 percent of youth received their high school diploma or GED certificate or were actively pursuing it
- 83 percent maintained stable housing after exiting the program
- 87 percent avoided any involvement with the criminal-justice system

First Place for Youth is also in the process of designing an external implementation-and-outcomes evaluation of its activities. Evidence from this review will be used to strengthen the First Place for Youth model.

PERFORMANCE

In 2010, First Place for Youth housed 275 youth. By 2013 the program had grown 50 percent to housing 404 youth. Ninety-one percent of youth involved in First Place for Youth enrolled in post-secondary education upon graduation from high school.

PLANS FOR GROWTH

First Place for Youth plans to house 700 by 2018, primarily by expanding its programs in the Los Angeles area. The organization is also considering expanding to an additional county within California, as well as nationally to two new sites.

FOR MORE INFORMATION, VISIT WWW.FIRSTPLACEFORYOUTH.ORG.

NATIONAL GUARD YOUTH CHALLENGE PROGRAM

The National Guard Youth ChalleNGe Program provides an intensive program to reengage high school dropouts aged 16–18 and get them back on track. The five-month residential program, often located at military bases, is anchored by a curriculum that promotes positive youth development. A twelve-month structured mentoring phase follows the residential phase. The program's key goals are to help young people further their education and get a foothold in the labor market.

EVIDENCE

In 2011, MDRC released final results of a multi-year study of ChalleNGe programs. The randomized controlled trial found that ChalleNGe had statistically significant impacts on GED receipt, employment, and earnings three years after youth entered the study. A cost-benefit analysis by the RAND Corporation—which utilized the impacts results—calculated that ChalleNGe admission generates labor-market earnings and other benefits of $2.66 for every dollar expended on the program and an estimated return on investment of 166 percent.

PERFORMANCE

Over 121,000 youth have graduated since the program began in 1993. Over 60 percent of the graduates—former high school dropouts—have earned their GED or high school diploma while in the program. Currently, ChalleNGe programs operate in thirty-five locations across twenty-seven states, plus the District of Columbia and Puerto Rico. These programs serve approximately nine thousand young people per year.

PLANS FOR GROWTH

ChalleNGe has a longer-term goal of serving more than double the number of youth per year than they currently do. In addition, the program is testing out an extension of the current ChalleNGe model, called Job ChalleNGe. Job ChalleNGe will build on the program's current components with more time and concentrated focus on improving program participants' employment outcomes.

FOR MORE INFORMATION, VISIT WWW.JOINTSERVICESSUPPORT.ORG/NGYCP/.

TEEN PREGNANCY PREVENTION INITIATIVE

United Way of Greater Milwaukee's Teen Pregnancy Prevention initiative invested in creative solutions to combat Milwaukee's teen-pregnancy epidemic.

The initiative utilized a comprehensive approach and formed partnerships with schools, hospitals, and other philanthropic organizations to raise awareness of the negative effects of teen pregnancy. The TPP initiative made national headlines for both its efficacy and its engaging and controversial public-awareness campaigns aimed at young people and their parents.

EVIDENCE

Data from the City of Milwaukee Health Department provided the 50 percent reduction figure. The health department credits the initiative for the city's unprecedented success.

According to an article in the *American Journal of Public Health*, "Milwaukee is leading the way in the fight with a successful community-based prevention program." United Way Worldwide, Mutual of America, and the White House Council for Community Solutions have all cited the Teen Pregnancy Prevention initiative for its groundbreaking, successful approach.

PERFORMANCE

By 2012, Milwaukee's teen-pregnancy rates fell by 50 percent. The initiative's original goal—46 percent reduction by 2015—was considered at the time to be one of the loftiest in the nation.

Teen pregnancies declined across every racial and ethnic group in Milwaukee. From 2006 to 2011, the abortion rate in Milwaukee County declined from 18.7 per 1,000 females aged eighteen or younger, to 13.2.

PLANS FOR GROWTH

The United Way of Greater Milwaukee continues to fund-raise and form new partnerships across all sectors in order to further the goals of the Teen Pregnancy Prevention initiative.

FOR MORE INFORMATION, VISIT WWW.UNITEDWAYMILWAUKEE.ORG/ TEENPREGNANCYPREVENTION.

YOUTH VILLAGES

Youth Villages puts America's most troubled youth on the road to a healthy and productive future. Youth Villages aims to help participants boost their academic achievement, avoid illegal activity, and attain regular employment. The program focuses its in-home and residential programs on youths up to age twenty-two, many of whom have cycled through the foster-care, juvenile-justice, or mental-health systems.

EVIDENCE

Youth Villages deploys over seventeen evidence-based protocols to ensure high-quality programming for disadvantaged young people. Compared with peer out-of-home service organizations, Youth Villages programs have success rates twice that of traditional services at one-third of their cost. A report by MDRC on the impacts of the Youth Villages Transitional Living program in Tennessee, which serves young adults aged 17–22 who have a history of involvement with the foster-care or juvenile-justice systems, or who otherwise find themselves unprepared for independent living, will be released in 2015.

PERFORMANCE

Beginning in 2005, Youth Villages served 10,542 youth. By 2013, the program more than doubled—serving 22,141 youth. In 2013, 80 percent of participants in Youth Villages' intensive in-home program lived successfully with their family, or independently, twelve months after discharge.

Two years after completing Youth Villages' programs, 82 percent of participants had no legal trouble, and 83 percent of participants were either in school, earning their GED, or graduated.

PLANS FOR GROWTH

In order to expand its service, Youth Villages plans to deepen relationships with state governments and form strategic partnerships with members of the business and nonprofit communities. In addition, Youth Villages will strengthen its national organization by bolstering its business-development and governmental-relations staff, leadership, and capacity.

FOR MORE INFORMATION, VISIT WWW.YOUTHVILLAGES.ORG.

ABOUT RESULTS FOR AMERICA

R esults for America, which launched in April 2012, seeks to improve outcomes for young people, their families, and communities by shifting public resources toward programs and practices that use evidence and data to improve quality and get better results.

Results for America seeks to drive broader systems-change so that "investing in what works" becomes the new norm for allocating public dollars.

FOR MORE INFORMATION, VISIT WWW.INVESTINWHATWORKS.ORG.

ABOUT THE EDITORS

Jim Nussle is founder and president of the Nussle Group. From 2007 to 2009, he served as director of the Office of Management and Budget in the White House. For the sixteen years prior, he represented southeastern Iowa in the United States Congress, where he served as chairman of the Budget Committee.

Peter Orszag is a vice chairman of corporate investment banking and chairman of the Financial Strategy and Solutions Group at Citigroup. From 2009 to 2010, he served as director of the Office of Management and Budget in the White House, and from 2007 to 2008 he was the director of the Congressional Budget Office (CBO).

ABOUT THE AUTHORS

Senator Kelly Ayotte is the junior senator from New Hampshire. She was New Hampshire's first female attorney general. She currently serves on the Senate Armed Services, Budget, Commerce, Homeland Security and Governmental Affairs, and Aging Committees.

Melody Barnes is a senior adviser of Albright Stonebridge Group and the CEO of Melody Barnes Solutions. From 2009 to 2011, she served as director of the White House Domestic Policy Council. Before that she was the executive vice president for the Center for American Progress and served as U.S. Senator Ted Kennedy's chief counsel on the Senate Judiciary Committee.

John Bridgeland is CEO of Civic Enterprises and co-chair of the Franklin Project at the Aspen Institute. He served in the Bush White House for all eight years, as director of the White House Domestic Policy Council, and as director of the USA Freedom Corps.

Michael Gerson is senior advisor to the ONE Campaign and a nationally syndicated columnist for the *Washington Post*. Until 2006, Gerson was a top aide to President George W. Bush as Assistant to the President for Policy and Strategic Planning.

Robert Gordon served as acting deputy director and executive associate director at the Office of Management and Budget, where he spearheaded OMB's effort to increase the use of evidence and evaluation across the federal government.

Ron Haskins is a senior fellow in the Economic Studies program and codirector of the Center on Children and Families at the Brookings Institution. In 2002, he was the senior adviser for welfare policy for President George W. Bush.

Glenn Hubbard is dean of Columbia Business School. From 2001 to 2003, he served as chairman of the Council of Economic Advisers. From 1991 to 1993 he was a deputy assistant secretary at the Treasury Department.

Michele Jolin is the founder and managing partner for Results for America. She is also senior fellow at the Center for American Progress. She served on President Obama's White House Council for Community Solutions and as chief of staff for President Clinton's Council of Economic Advisers.

Kevin Madden is a Republican political strategist. He was most recently a senior adviser to Governor Mitt Romney's presidential campaign in 2012 and served as national press secretary for the governor's 2008 campaign.

Raj Shah is the founder and managing partner of Latitude Capital, a global emerging markets power and infrastructure private equity firm and a Distinguished Fellow at the Georgetown University School of Foreign Service. Shah served as Administrator of the United States Agency for International Development (USAID) from January 2010 to February 2015.

Gene Sperling served as the director of the National Economic Council for both President Clinton and President Obama. He also served as counselor to Treasury Secretary Tim Geithner and as chief economic adviser to Hillary Clinton's 2008 presidential campaign.

Senator Mark Warner is the senior senator from Virginia. Before that, he served four years as governor of Virginia. He currently serves on the Senate Finance, Banking, Budget, and Intelligence Committees.

Howard Wolfson served as New York City's deputy mayor for government affairs and communications from 2010 to 2013. During the 2008 presidential campaign, he worked as Hillary Clinton's co-chief strategist and communications director.

ACKNOWLEDGMENTS

Special thanks to the following foundations for making all the work of Results for America possible: the Laura and John Arnold Foundation, Bloomberg Philanthropies, the Annie E. Casey Foundation, the Edna McConnell Clark Foundation, the William and Flora Hewlett Foundation, the George Kaiser Family Foundation and Mario Morino.

We also would like to thank our partners at the Bridgespan Group, Civic Enterprises, MDRC, West Wing Writers, and the Pew Charitable Trusts for their ongoing thought partnership to our team.

A very special thanks to Rob Ivry and Robert Gordon for their meticulous review of our manuscript—their thoughtful eye strengthened the rigor and quality of our book and for that we are extremely appreciative.

Finally, to Dylan Loewe, for his enthusiasm for and commitment to dissecting complex ideas and presenting them in the most interesting and convincing ways, and making these ideas accessible to as many readers as possible. And, thank you to Shivam Mallick Shah for leading and orchestrating the creation of this book with great strategic insight, clarity of thinking, wisdom, and the good humor she brings to everything she does.

Michele Jolin
Results for America

NOTES

PREFACE

1   Kerry Searle Grannis and Isabel V. Sawhill, "Improving
    Children's Life Chances: Estimates from the Social Genome
    Model," Social Genome Project Research 49 (Brookings
    Institution, 2013), http://www.brookings.edu/research/
    papers/2013/10/11-improving-childrens-life-chances-
    sawhill-grannis.

CHAPTER I.

2   Michael Lewis, *Moneyball: The Art of Winning an Unfair
    Game* (New York: W. W. Norton, 2003).

3   In June 2013, the Atlantic magazine published an article
    called "Can Government Play Moneyball" by Peter Orszag
    and John Bridgeland, who are both contributors to this book.
    This chapter is based, in part, on ideas first articulated in
    that article. And that article is the inspiration for this book.

4   Congressional Budget Office, Office of Management and
    Budget, *Historical Budget Data—August 2013*, August 12,
    2013, http://www.cbo.gov/sites/default/files/cbofiles/
    attachments/HistoricalBudgetData_Aug13.pdf.

5   Ron Haskins and Jon Baron, *Building the Connection between Policy and Evidence*, National Endowment for Society, Technology, and the Arts (UK), September 2011, http://coalition4evidence.org/wp-content/uploads/uploads-dupes-safety/Haskins-Baron-paper-on-fed-evid-based-initiatives-2011.pdf.

6   Visit on the web at http://www.nursefamilypartnership.org/.

7   Amanda Terkel, "112th Congress Set to Become Most Unproductive Since 1940s," *Huffington Post*, December 28, 2012, http://www.huffingtonpost.com/2012/12/28/congress-unproductive_n_2371387.html.

8   McKinsey & Company, Social Sector Office, *The Economic Impact of the Achievement Gap in America's Schools*, April 2009, http://mckinseyonsociety.com/downloads/reports/Education/achievement_gap_report.pdf.

9   American Civil Liberties Union, *Smart Reform Is Possible: States Reducing Incarceration Rates and Costs While Protecting Communities*, August 2011, https://www.aclu.org/files/assets/smartreformispossible.pdf.

10   NAEP Data Explorer, http://nces.ed.gov/nationsreportcard/naepdata/.

11   Sophia Kerby, "The Top 10 Most Startling Facts About People of Color and Criminal Justice in the United States: A Look at the Racial Disparities Inherent in Our Nation's Criminal-Justice System," on the website of the Center for American Progress, March 13, 2012, http://www.

americanprogress.org/issues/race/news/2012/03/13/11351/
the-top-10-most-startling-facts-about-people-of-color-and-
criminal-justice-in-the-united-states/.

CHAPTER II.

12   Frederick Mosteller, "The Tennessee Study of Class Size
in the Early School Grades," *Critical Issues for Children
and Youths* 5, no. 2 (Summer/Fall 1995): 113–27, https://
www.princeton.edu/futureofchildren/publications/
docs/05_02_08.pdf.

13   Matthew M. Chingos and Grover J. "Russ" Whitehurst,
"Class Size: What Research Says and What It Means for State
Policy," Brookings Institution, May 11, 2011, http://www.
brookings.edu/research/papers/2011/05/11-class-size-
whitehurst-chingos.

14   Susan Dynarski, Joshua M. Hyman, and Diane Whitmore
Schanzenbach, "Experimental Evidence on the Effect of
Childhood Investments on Postsecondary Attainment and
Degree Completion," (NBER Working Paper No. 17533,
National Bureau of Economic Research, October 2011,
revised July 12, 2013), http://www.nber.org/papers/w17533.

15   Caroline M. Hoxby, "The Effects of Class Size on Student
Achievement: New Evidence from Population Variation,"
Quarterly Journal of Economics 115, no. 4 (November 2000):

1239–85, http://qje.oxfordjournals.org/content/115/4/1239. abstract.

16   "Smarter Lunchrooms," on the website of the Cornell University Food and Brand Lab, last modified June 20, 2013, http://www.foodpsychology.cornell.edu/research/smarter-lunchrooms.html.

17   The National Bureau of Economic Research, *Economic Report of the President*, March 2014, http://www.nber.org/erp/2014_economic_report_of_the_president.pdf.

18   Jim Manzi, *Uncontrolled: The Surprising Payoff of Trial-and-Error for Business, Politics, and Society* (New York: Basic Books, 2012).

19   Much of the evidence cited in this section is included in a 2014 White House report, which the author supervised as director of the National Economic Council: "Increasing College Opportunity for Low-Income Students: Promising Models and a Call to Action," January 2014.

CHAPTER III.

20   Julia B. Isaacs, Isabel V. Sawhill, and Ron Haskins, *Getting Ahead or Losing Ground: Economic Mobility in America*, Brookings Institution, February 2008, p. 19, http://www.brookings.edu/~/media/research/files/reports/2008/2/economic%20mobility%20sawhill/02_economic_mobility_sawhill.pdf.

21   Caroline Hoxby and Christopher Avery, "The Missing 'One-Offs': The Hidden Supply of High-Achieving, Low-Income Students," *Brookings Papers on Economic Activity*, Spring 2013, p. 26, http://www.brookings.edu/~/media/projects/bpea/spring%202013/2013a_hoxby.pdf.

22   Amanda Pallais, "Small Differences that Matter: Mistakes in Applying to College" (SEII Discussion Paper #2014.02, School Effectiveness and Inequality Initiative, MIT, April 2014), 2-3, http://seii.mit.edu/wp-content/uploads/2014/04/SEII-Discussion-Paper-2014.02-Pallais2.pdf.

23   Caroline Hoxby and Sarah Turner, "Expanding College Opportunities for High-Achieving, Low Income Students" (SIEPR Discussion Paper No. 12-014, Stanford Institute for Economic Policy Research, Stanford University, March 2013), 24, http://siepr.stanford.edu/?q=/system/files/shared/pubs/papers/12-014paper.pdf.

24   Benjamin L. Castleman and Lindsay C. Page, "Summer Nudging: Can Personalized Text Messages and Peer Mentor Outreach Increase College Going Among Low-Income High School Graduates?" (EdPolicyWorks Working Paper Series No. 9, University of Virginia, updated January 2014), 2, http://curry.virginia.edu/uploads/resourceLibrary/9_Castleman_SummerTextMessages.pdf.

25   Students in College Track, which provides comprehensive services from ninth grade through college, graduate from

college at 2.5 times the rate of low-income youth nationally (College Track, "Our Results," http://collegetrack.org/why-it-matters/our-results/). Another study found that 85 percent of I Have a Dream alumni in New York City who completed high school have enrolled in college, much higher than the 64 percent average across the city (Arete Consulting, "'I Have a Dream' Foundation New York Metro: Program Evaluation Report," January 2010, p. 4, http://www.socialimpactexchange.org/sites/www.socialimpactexchange.org/files/IHDF-NY%20Metro%20Program%20Evaluation%20Report%202010.pdf). Posse has been able to get students with SAT scores of 1050 to colleges with average SAT scores of 1350 *and have over 90 percent of them graduate from those colleges* (Posse Foundation, "Fulfilling the Promise: The Impact of Posse After 20 Years," 2012, p. 8, http://www.possefoundation.org/m/alum-report-web.pdf). Lastly, GEAR UP has seen success across the country: first-year postsecondary attendance for participants in Washington State was nearly 70 percent higher than a comparison group, and the West Virginia GEAR UP program led the number of low-income youths seeking information about financial aid for college to rise from 24 percent to 81 percent in the first three years. These are just a few of the headlines about results that hold such promise for the future.

26   Trudi Renwick, "What is the Supplemental Poverty
        Measure and How Does it Differ from the Official
        Measure?," *Random Samplings* (blog), U.S. Census Bureau,
        November 5, 2013, http://blogs.census.gov/2013/11/05/
        what-is-the-supplemental-poverty-measure-and-how-does-
        it-differ-from-the-official-measure-2/.

27   "About Experimental Measures," on the website of the
        United States Census Bureau, last modified January 13, 2011,
        https://www.census.gov/hhes/povmeas/about/index.html.
        The Interagency Technical Working Group on Developing a
        Supplemental Poverty Measure was formed in 2009.

28   Liana Fox et al., "Waging War on Poverty: Historical Trends
        in Poverty Using the Supplemental Poverty Measure" (CPRC
        Working Paper. No. 13-02, Columbia Population Research
        Center, December 2013), http://socialwork.columbia.
        edu/sites/default/files/file_manager/pdfs/News/Fox_
        Waging%20War%20on%20Poverty_dec13.pdf.

29   Arloc Sherman, "Official Poverty Measure Masks Gains
        Made Over Last 50 Years," on the website of the Center on
        Budget and Policy Priorities, September 13, 2013, http://
        www.cbpp.org/cms/?fa=view&id=4015.

30   Liana Fox et al., "Waging War on Poverty: Historical Trends in Poverty Using the Supplemental Poverty Measure" (CPRC Working Paper. No. 13-02, Columbia Population Research Center, December 2013), http://socialwork.columbia.edu/sites/default/files/file_manager/pdfs/News/Fox_Waging%20War%20on%20Poverty_dec13.pdf.

31   Ibid.

32   Margot L. Crandall-Hollick, *The American Opportunity Tax Credit: Overview, Analysis, and Policy Options*, Congressional Research Service, July 28,2014, p. 23, http://fas.org/sgp/crs/misc/R42561.pdf. The Child Tax Credit is calculated based on AGI.

33   "Child Tax Credit," on the website of the Tax Policy Center, http://www.taxpolicycenter.org/taxtopics/encyclopedia/child-tax-credit.cfm.

34   Executive Office of the President and U.S. Treasury Department, *The President's Proposal to Expand the Earned Income Tax Credit*, March 2014, p. 4, http://www.whitehouse.gov/sites/default/files/docs/eitc_report.pdf.

35   Crandall-Hollick, *American Opportunity Tax Credit*, 1.

36   Chuck Marr, Chye-Ching Huang, and Arloc Sherman, *Earned Income Tax Credit Promotes Work, Encourages Children's Success at School, Research Finds: For Children, Research Indicates that Work, Income, and Health Benefits Extend Into Adulthood*, Center on Budget and Policy

Priorities, revised April 15, 2014, http://www.cbpp.org/
cms/?fa=view&id=3793.

37   Bruce D. Meyer and Dan T. Rosenbaum, "Welfare, the
     Earned Income Tax Credit, and the Labor Supply of Single
     Mothers," *Quarterly Journal of Economics* 116, no. 3 (August
     2001): 1083, 1101, http://www.ssc.wisc.edu/~scholz/
     Teaching_742/Meyer_Rosenbaum.pdf.

38   Nada Eissa and Jeffrey B. Liebman, "Labor Supply Response
     to the Earned Income Tax Credit," *Quarterly Journal of
     Economics* 111, no. 2 (1996): 605–37, http://www.hks.harvard.
     edu/jeffreyliebman/eissaliebmanqje.pdf.

39   Bruce D. Meyer, "The Effects of the Earned Income Tax
     Credit and Recent Reforms," *Tax Policy and the Economy* 24
     (August 2010): 175, http://www.nber.org/chapters/c11973.
     pdf.

40   Yonatan Ben-Shalom, Robert Moffitt, and John Karl
     Scholz, "An Assessment of the Effectiveness of Anti-Poverty
     Programs in the United States" (IRP Discussion Paper no.
     1392-11, Institute for Research on Poverty, June 2010, revised
     May 2011), 28, http://www.ssc.wisc.edu/~scholz/Research/
     Effectiveness.pdf.

41   Meyer, "Effects," 168.

42   "US Business Cycle Expansions and Contractions,"
     on the website of the National Bureau of Economic Research,
     http://www.nber.org/cycles.html. Recession ended in
     March 1991.

CHAPTER IV.

43 John Enders, Associated Press, "Sunnyvale's 'Results-Oriented' Budget Innovations Win National Praise," *Los Angeles Times*, September 12, 1993, http://articles.latimes.com/1993-09-12/local/me-34303_1_employee-performance.

44 Martin Kasindorf, "Clinton Tours Town He Calls Role Model," *Newsday*, September 11, 1993.

45 Clinton T. Brass , *Changes to the Government Performance and Results Act (GPRA): Overview of the New Framework of Products and Processes*, Congressional Research Service, February 29, 2012, http://fas.org/sgp/crs/misc/R42379.pdf.

46 "OMB's Program Assessment Rating Tool (PART)," on the website of Strategisys, http://strategisys.com/omb_part.

47 U.S. Government Accountability Office, *Multiple Employment and Training Programs: Providing Information on Colocating Services and Consolidating Administrative Structures Could Promote Efficiencies*, January 2011, http://www.gao.gov/new.items/d1192.pdf.

48 U.S. Government Accountability Office, *Workforce Investment Act: Strategies Needed to Improve Certain Training Outcome Data*, January 2014, p. 17, http://www.workforcedqc.org/sites/default/files/images/GAO%20Report-WIA%20Strategies%20to%20Improve%20Outcome%20Data.pdf.

49   Jim Manzi, *Uncontrolled: The Surprising Payoff of Trial-and-Error for Business, Politics, and Society* (New York: Basic Books, 2012).

50   Scott Cody and Andrew Asher, *Proposal 14: Smarter, Better, Faster: The Potential for Predictive Analytics and Rapid-Cycle Evaluation to Improve Program Development and Outcomes*, the Hamilton Project and the Brookings Institution, http://www.brookings.edu/~/media/research/files/papers/2014/06/19_hamilton_policies_addressing_poverty/predictive_analytics_rapid_cycle_evaluation_cody_asher.pdf.

51   Roger Jay Dilger and Richard S. Beth, *Unfunded Mandates Reform Act: History, Impact, and Issues*, Congressional Research Service, http://fas.org/sgp/crs/misc/R40957.pdf. See p. 20.

52   Social Impact Bonds are gaining momentum across the United States. New York City, New York State, Massachusetts, and Utah are currently operating Social Impact Bond models. The Obama administration began implementing Pay for Success efforts in FY 2012 using existing authorities.

CHAPTER V.

53   Stephanie Condon, "Poll: Most Tea Party Supporters Say Their Taxes Are Fair," CBS News, April 14, 2010, http://www.cbsnews.com/news/poll-most-tea-party-supporters-say-their-taxes-are-fair/.

54   CBS News/New York Times, *The Tea Party Movement: What They Think*, April 14, 2010, http://www.cbsnews.com/htdocs/pdf/poll_tea_party_041410.pdf.

55   Brian Montopoli, "Tea Party Supporters: Who They Are and What They Believe," CBS News, December 14, 2012, http://www.cbsnews.com/news/tea-party-supporters-who-they-are-and-what-they-believe/.

56   "Primary Resources: Acceptance of the Republican Nomination for President," on the website of American Experience, Public Broadcasting Service, http://www.pbs.org/wgbh/americanexperience/features/primary-resources/reagan-nomination/.

57   Pew Research Center, "Views of Government: Key Data Points," October 22, 2013, http://www.pewresearch.org/key-data-points/views-of-government-key-data-points/

58   Pew Research Center, *Millennials in Adulthood: Detached from Institutions, Networked with Friends*, March 2014, http://www.pewsocialtrends.org/files/2014/03/2014-03-07_generations-report-version-for-web.pdf.

CHAPTER VI.

59   John F. Kennedy, "Special Message to the Congress on
      Foreign Aid," March 22, 1961, on the website of the American
      Presidency Project, http://www.presidency.ucsb.edu/
      ws/?pid=8545.

60   Richard Nixon, "Special Message to the Congress on
      Foreign Aid," May 28, 1969, on the website of the American
      Presidency Project, http://www.presidency.ucsb.edu/
      ws/?pid=2073.

61   *Child Survival: The Unfinished Agenda to Reduce Global Child
      Mortality—Hearing Before the Subcommittee on Africa and
      Global Health of the Committee on Foreign Affairs, House
      Of Representatives*, 110th Congress, Second Session, p. 10
      (March 13, 2008), statement of Kent R. Hill, Assistant
      Administrator, Bureau for Global Health, U.S. Agency for
      International Development, http://www.gpo.gov/fdsys/pkg/
      CHRG-110hhrg41233/pdf/CHRG-110hhrg41233.pdf.

62   "Deworm the World Initiative," on the website of Evidence
      Action, http://www.evidenceaction.org/deworm-the-world/.

63   "Lifebuoy's 1 Billion Ambition," on the website of Unilever,
      https://www.unilever.com/sustainable-living/the-
      sustainable-living-plan/improving-health-and-well-being/
      health-and-hygiene/changing-hygiene-habits-for-better-
      health/Lifebuoys-one-billion-ambition.html.

64   Ibid.

65   Alexis Okeowo, "Rick Warren in Rwanda," n+1, August 18, 2010, https://nplusonemag.com/online-only/online-only/rick-warren-in-rwanda/.

66   World Health Organization, "WHO/UNICEF Report: Malaria MDG Target Achieved Amid Sharp Drop in Cases and Mortality, but 3 Billion People Remain at Risk," news release, September 17, 2015, http://www.who.int/mediacentre/news/releases/2015/malaria-mdg-target/en/.

67   World Health Organization, "Tuberculosis: Fact Sheet No. 104," updated October 2015, http://www.who.int/mediacentre/factsheets/fs104/en/.

68   *Words of Wisdom: P. J. O' Rourke* (Students' Academy, 2014), eBook.

69   "World AIDS Day 2014 Update: PEPFAR Latest Results Fact Sheet," on the website of the United States President's Emergency Plan for AIDS Relief, http://www.pepfar.gov/funding/results/.

70   L. M. Heaton et al., "Estimating the Impact of the U.S. President's Emergency Plan for AIDS Relief on HIV Treatment and Prevention Programmes in Africa," National Center for Biotechnology Information, June 8, 2015, http://www.ncbi.nlm.nih.gov/pubmed/26056389.

71   J. H. Choi and M. A. Croyle, "Emerging Targets and Novel Approaches to Ebola Virus Prophylaxis and Treatment," BioDrugs 27, no. 6 (December 2013): 565–83, on the website of the National Center for Biotechnology Information, http://www.ncbi.nlm.nih.gov/pubmed/23813435.

72   Ana Maria Henao-Restrepo et al., "Efficacy and Effectiveness
      of an rVSV-Vectored Vaccine Expressing Ebola Surface
      Glycoprotein: Interim Results from the Guinea Ring
      Vaccination Cluster-Randomised Trial," The Lancet 386, no.
      9996 (August 3, 2015): 829–930, http://www.thelancet.com/
      journals/lancet/article/PIIS0140-6736(15)61117-5/abstract.

73   Suzanne Goldenberg, "Africa Famine: Soaring Food Prices
      Intensifying Crisis, Report Warns," The Guardian, August
      16, 2011, http://www.theguardian.com/environment/2011/
      aug/16/africa-famine-food-prices-world-bank.

74   USAID, "U.S. Government Announces Child Stunting
      Rates Drop in Ethiopia, Maize Yields Increase in
      Zambia," news release, November 6, 2014, https://
      www.usaid.gov/news-information/press-releases/
      nov-6-2014-us-government-announces-child-stunting-
      rates-drop-ethiopia-maize.

75   "Egypt," on the website of USAID, https://www.usaid.gov/
      egypt.

76   "Afghanistan: Primary Health Care," on the website of
      the World Health Organization Regional Office for the
      Eastern Mediterranean," http://www.emro.who.int/afg/
      programmes/primary-health-care-phc.html.

77   "Afghanistan: Education," on the website of USAID, https://
      www.usaid.gov/afghanistan/education.

78   World Health Organization, "Ebola Data and Statistics,"
      October 22, 2015, http://apps.who.int/gho/data/view.ebola-

sitrep.ebola-summary-20151022?lang=en; see also "Ebola in Graphics: The Toll of a Tragedy."

79 "2014 Ebola Outbreak in West Africa—Case Counts," Centers for Disease Control and Prevention, updated November 5, 2015, http://www.cdc.gov/vhf/ebola/outbreaks/2014-west-africa/case-counts.html#modalIdString_cases-localized-transmission.

80 Ibid.

81 Ibid.

CHAPTER VII.

82 Dylan Matthews, "Graph of the Day: Congress Is Less Popular Than Lice, Colonoscopies and Nickelback," *Wonkblog, Washington Post*, January 10, 2013, http://www.washingtonpost.com/blogs/wonkblog/wp/2013/01/10/graph-of-the-day-congress-is-less-popular-than-lice-colonoscopies-and-nickelback/.

AFTERWORD

83 All views expressed in this afterword are solely those of authors Robert Gordon and Ron Haskins.

84 Cass R. Sunstein, "The Office of Information and Regulatory Affairs: Myths and Realities" (Harvard Public Law Working Paper No. 13-07, December 21, 2012, revised February 12,

2013), http://papers.ssrn.com/sol3/papers.cfm?abstract_
id=2192639.

85   Visit on the web at http://www.pewtrusts.org/en/projects/
pew-macarthur-results-first-initiative.

86   Max Stier, *A More Efficient and Effective Government:
Cultivating the Federal Workforce*, written testimony prepared
for the Senate Committee on Homeland Security and
Governmental Affairs Subcommittee on the Efficiency and
Effectiveness of Federal Programs and the Federal Workforce,
Partnership for Public Service, May 6, 2014, http://
ourpublicservice.org/OPS/publications/viewcontentdetails.
php?id=242.

87   U.S. Government Accountability Office, *Federal Workers:
Results of Studies on Federal Pay Varied Due to Differing
Methodologies*, June 2012, 42, fig. 5, http://www.gao.gov/
assets/600/591817.pdf.

88   Stier, *A More Efficient and Effective Government*.

89   Partnership for Public Service and Booz Allen Hamilton,
Building the Enterprise: A New Civil Service Framework,
April 2014, http://ourpublicservice.org/OPS/publications/
viewcontentdetails.php?id=237.

90   Ron Haskins, *Show Me the Results: Obama's Fight for Rigor
and Evidence in Social Policy* (Washington, DC: Brookings
Institution Press, 2014).

91   Carolyn Heinrich, Peter R. Mueser, Kenneth R. Troske,
Jacom M. Benus, et al., *Workforce Investment Act Non-
Experimental Net Impact Evaluation*, IMPAQ International,

http://wdr.doleta.gov/research/FullText_Documents/
Workforce%20Investment%20Act%20Non-
Experimental%20Net%20Impact%20Evaluation%20-%20
Final%20Report.pdf.

92   U.S. Department of Education Press Office, "U.S.
Department of Education Announces Highest-
Rated Applications for Investing in Innovation 2013
Competition," on the website of the U.S. Department of
Education, November 8, 2013, http://www.ed.gov/news/
press-releases/us-department-education-announces-
highest-rated-applications-investing-innovatio.

93   "Pay-For-Performance Act: Senate Introduces Treasury
Incentive Fund Bill," on the website of the Nonprofit
Finance Fund, http://payforsuccess.org/resources/
pay-performance-act-senate-introduces-treasury-incentive-
fund-bill; "Representatives Young & Delaney Introduce
Social Impact Bond Act," on the website of the Nonprofit
Finance Fund, http://payforsuccess.org/resources/
representatives-young-delaney-introduce-social-impact-
bond-act.

94   Michael Puma et al., *Head Start Impact Study: Final Report,
Executive Summary*, U.S. Department of Health and Human
Services, Administration for Children and Families, January
15, 2010, http://www.acf.hhs.gov/programs/opre/resource/
head-start-impact-study-final-report-executive-summary.

95   U.S. Department of Health and Human Services,
Administration for Children and Families, Office of Head

Start, *Head Start Program Performance Standards*, 45 CFR Chapter XIII, October 1, 2009, https://eclkc.ohs.acf.hhs.gov/hslc/standards/hspps/45-cfr-chapter-xiii/45-cfr-chap-xiii-eng.pdf.

96   Sara Mead, *Renewing Head Start's Promise: Invest in What Works for Disadvantaged Preschoolers*, Results for America and Bellwether Education Partners, July 2014, http://bellwethereducation.org/publication/RenewingHeadStartsPromise.

97   "Executive Order 13563—Improving Regulation and Regulatory Review," on the website of the White House Office of the Press Secretary, January 18, 2011, http://www.whitehouse.gov/the-press-office/2011/01/18/improving-regulation-and-regulatory-review-executive-order.

98   David H. Autor and Mark Duggan, *Supporting Work: A Proposal for Modernizing the U.S. Disability Insurance System*, Center for American Progress and the Hamilton Project, December 2010, http://www.brookings.edu/~/media/research/files/papers/2010/12/disability%20insurance%20autor/12_disability_insurance_autor.pdf.

99   Jeffrey B. Liebman and Jack A. Smalligan, *Proposal 4: An Evidence-Based Path to Disability Insurance Reform*, Hamilton Project, Brookings Institution, February 2013, http://www.hamiltonproject.org/files/downloads_and_links/THP_15WaysFedBudget_Prop4.pdf.

100   Results for America and the Hamilton Project, Brookings Institution, *Investing in What Works: The Importance of Evidence-Based Policymaking*, April 17, 2013, http://www. hamiltonproject.org/events/investing_in_what_works_the_ importance_of_evidence-based_policymaking.

101   White House Office of Management and Budget, *Fiscal Year 2013: Cuts, Consolidations, and Savings; Budget of the U.S. Government*, http://www.whitehouse.gov/sites/default/ files/omb/budget/fy2013/assets/ccs.pdf.

GPM matrix - Applies Money ball for govt.

p. 6 - 3 principals / p. 45 also /

p. 8 window of opportunity

p. 13 Healthier people more productive/earn more

p. 25 Goal of public policy to improve lives // presentation of the problem (challenge, evidence based solutions, call to action)

p. 155 - Changing the internal instinct (org) to avoid risk was probably the greatest obstacle (to chg)

p. 156 - Lessons learned
   1) Private sector principals apply
   2) Create collaborative risk taking environment
   3) Can build political (Congressional) support

p. 169 Even when we have good evidence (measured), The story of what works is incomplete. (attribution reasons/causes)

p. 170 - Need better definitions.

p. 171 Joint PPPs

p. 180 Lessons learned for social sector

Made in the USA
Middletown, DE
11 November 2016